Dr. Roger L. Frye

PATHWAY
to *Freedom*

Discover Your God-Given
Destiny Through Christ

Pathway to Freedom
Original Copyright © 2015 by Roger L. Frye

Published by:
Latte Media Group
1030 E. Hwy 377 Suite 110 Box 184
Granbury, TX 76048
www.LatteBros.com

All rights reserved. No part of this book may be reproduced in any form whatsoever, except for brief quotations, without the written permission of the publisher.

Unless otherwise noted, all Scripture quotations are taken from the New King James Version. Copyright © 1979, 1980, 1982, by Thomas Nelson, Inc. Used by permission. All rights reserved.

Scripture taken from the HOLY BIBLE, NEW INTERNATIONAL VERSION. Copyright © 1973, 1978, 1984 International Bible Society. Used by permission of Zondervan Bible Publishers.

Cover Design by Greg Solomon

ISBN-978-0-9834869-5-4

Printed in the United States of America.

Disclaimer

Pathway to Freedom does not seek to be in conflict with any medical or psychiatric practices. The information here is intended for your spiritual growth and general knowledge. It is not intended to be a substitute for medical or psychiatric advice or treatment for specific medical or psychological conditions or disorders.

Contents

iii	Disclaimer
vii	ACKNOWLEDGEMENTS
1	CHAPTER ONE
	1 *Preparing Your Heart*
5	CHAPTER TWO
	5 *Trap Number One: Hidden Sins*
25	CHAPTER THREE
	25 *Trap Number Two: Unforgiveness*
35	CHAPTER FOUR
	35 *Trap Number Three: Inner Vows and Judgments, Lies, and Expectancies*
43	CHAPTER FIVE
	43 *Trap Number Four: Soul Ties and Trauma Bonds*
49	CHAPTER SIX
	49 *Trap Number Five: Occultic Influence*
69	CHAPTER SEVEN
	69 *Trap Number Six: Curses*
85	CHAPTER EIGHT
	85 *Trap Number Seven: Trauma*
109	CHAPTER NINE
	109 *Freedom From Evil Spirits*
123	APPENDIX
139	ENDNOTES

ACKNOWLEDGEMENTS

I wish to express my deepest gratitude to my mentors over the years who have allowed me to soak up their wisdom and knowledge in the ministry of setting the captives free.

I want to say thank you to my friend, Carol Ties, for volunteering to use her editing and formatting skills for the glory of God. She was indeed an answer to prayer.

I want to say thank you to Sheree Bates for her ability to see the minute details where editing changes had to take place.

I want to say thank you to my good friend and "son" in the faith, Greg Solomon, who worked with me to create the cover design and added helpful suggestions along the way.

And finally, special thanks goes to my pastor, Mike Phillips, who possesses an unabashed passion for the freedom ministry of Pathway Church of Farmersville, TX and for the dear members there who hunger for the manifest presence of Almighty God.

Dr. Roger L. Frye

PATHWAY
to *Freedom*

Discover Your God-Given
Destiny Through Christ

CHAPTER ONE

Preparing Your Heart

I, Roger Frye, am the founder and president of Pathway to Freedom Ministries, the Freedom Ministry of Pathway Church, International. The contents of this book represent the information and ministry involved in our Encounter seminar. As you read, imagine yourself in attendance at one of these seminars, soaking up all that God has for you. If you have never attended a seminar, when reference is made to the prayer or action of the leader, you may want to enlist a trusted Christian prayer warrior who can say these prayers over you, or, if you prefer, you may contact our office to set up a personal ministry session.

I want to welcome each and every one of you to what we call "Encounter." Encounter is our introductory workshop that provides you the ability to make a giant step forward towards living the life of freedom Christ has for His children. Some of the things said in this seminar may stir up some strong reactions. It might even make you mad. If you find yourself getting angry, don't write off the whole workshop but put those concepts on the shelf to examine more closely at a later time. Someone once said, "You have to get mad before you can get glad." and I suppose, that in many cases, that saying is true. At least, I've seen this scenario play out in my own life at times.

Let me tell you a little about my own journey. I was age 20, almost 21 when I had a "born again" experience as I surrendered my life to my Lord and Savior, Jesus Christ. Although I was raised in a Christian home where we went to church three times a week and had family devotions every night after supper, I rebelled against all I was taught and chose to live a life of drugs, alcohol, witchcraft and sexual sin. But late one night years ago, as I lay in my bed, I felt broken and perplexed. I literally could not count to 10 without getting confused. I had wrecked my new Camaro, was about ready to lose my job, my girlfriend dumped me, and my body shook with what may have been a form of delirium tremens. In the midst of my despair I called out to Jesus and surrendered to His Lordship. He radically changed my life and all I wanted to do was read my Bible and tell people about Jesus. I was flying high and in love with Jesus.

But as time went by, some of the old sins and bondages began to resurface. I didn't understand why, so I just tried harder, studied harder, pushed myself harder, to make myself conform to my image of a true Christian. In reality, all of these religious activities did nothing to bring joy and freedom in my heart. I went to Bible College where I met Ruthie, my wife. From there I went to Seminary, hoping that through more Biblical knowledge I would be fulfilled and learn to walk in my destiny.

Perhaps you have gone to church regularly, read your Bible faithfully, memorized Scripture and prayed and prayed and prayed. You've gone to every "How-to" seminar that came to town, you've read the Christian self-help books, practiced fasting and self-denial, received prayer from healing gurus, and wept before the altar repeatedly only to see that, at the end of the day, the same sins and bondages, the besetting sins, the weaknesses, the Achilles heel, the failings, the sadness, the depression, the shame, the whatever, is still there. It's like you're stuck in some areas of your life and you're tired of trying to change.

A YouTube clip has been going around for some time. It depicts Bob Newhart as a psychologist using a unique form of therapy. A woman sets an appointment with him. He tells her his sessions only last five minutes and only costs five dollars. He starts her allotted five minutes, she tells him her problem which is the intense, crippling fear of being buried alive in a box, he asks her if she's ever been buried before in a box and she says no. He informs her that she has claustrophobia and she agrees. He promises her the cure in just two words. She takes out her note pad so she won't forget. He says that most people remember the two words. He looks at her and shouts, "Stop it!" He says the same thing several times in different ways. (We show this clip to the Encounter audience.) It's a funny routine but the truth is that most Christians have tried this method of mustering up their willpower to overcome their unwanted issues only to wind up in frustration. If you could have just "stopped it" you would have done so a long time ago.

Hear me brothers and sisters, God didn't mean for you to live in defeat. God meant for you to live the abundant life of freedom. This freedom does not come through your own effort and striving to perform. It comes through the power of the Holy Spirit enabling you to systematically dislodge you from the traps the enemy has set for your soul. In this Encounter seminar we explain the seven different traps and we come alongside you to pray for your release so that you may walk the pathway of freedom.

I love the name of this ministry, "Pathway to Freedom." This name implies process. It's a pathway, not a quick fix. Don't approach this subject hoping for an instant cure that enables you to live a carefree life, happily ever after. Typically, our freedom comes in layers, much like pealing an onion, but going through this seminar or reading this book will catapult you to a new level of victory.

To live the abundant life Christ offers doesn't mean that you never have problems, but it means that you live victoriously in and through whatever troubles you face. The Christian life is much like the picture portrayed in the Old Testament of the

Children of Israel. They lived in bondage in Egypt, a picture of our life before Christ. They served Pharaoh, a picture of Satan, the god of this age. The lamb was slain and the blood placed on the doors of those that believed so that the angel of destruction passed over and only afflicted those without the blood on the doorposts of their homes. The applied blood represents a picture of the sacrificial work of Christ on the Cross. Those who believe in Him are "under the blood" and safe from eternal destruction. Likewise, the crossing of the Red Sea pictures baptism. Because of unbelief the Children of Israel wandered around in the wilderness for 40 years, unable to walk in their destiny. Canaan was their goal. Canaan is not a picture of heaven, it is a picture of the fullness of life, of living in one's birthright. But once the Children of Israel got into Canaan, the Promised Land, there were battles to fight and victories to be won.

Many Christians mistakenly think that once they are able to get to that place where they're walking in their destiny, that there will be no more battles to fight. Picture a man who is tied to a chair with a gag over his mouth. His abuser is beating him ruthlessly causing the man's face to bruise, bleed and swell. The abuser slips out of the room for a minute and while he is gone, another man walks in and cuts the ropes that tied the bedraggled man down. Did the other man cut him free only so that he could escape? No, he also cut him free so that he could fight.

You need to be free so that you can fight the good fight of faith. When some of you really get free, the devil's going to be sorry for what he's done to you for so long. We're going to teach you some principles and we're going to pray for you so that you can get up off that chair, stand in the power of God, and fight the good fight of faith, not simply for your own survival, but for the freedom of those around you.

CHAPTER TWO

Trap Number One: Hidden Sins

Confession and repentance represent the first giant step in gaining freedom. The reason is that un-confessed, un-repented of sin provides an open door for the enemy to get into our lives and bring us into bondage. Our loving heavenly Father does not want us to live bound up but He earnestly desires that we live in freedom. The good news is that our God is very quick to forgive but He waits for us to confess. In 1 John 1:9 we read, *If we confess our sins He is faithful and just to forgive us our sins and to cleanse us from all unrighteousness.* Notice that the condition of forgiveness is that we confess. The word confess in the original Greek language means "to say the same thing." Biblical confession is to say the same thing that God says about our sin.

You will never find an incident in the Bible where God committed Himself to forgive sins that were not confessed. If you are uneasy about some specific activity or attitude, be honest about it. Don't call it by some modern psycho-babble term. Call it what God calls it because God forgives only what we admit is sin. He never agrees to forgive our "problems" or our "tendencies" or our "proclivities." If you have a "tendency" to lust, call it by its name- the sin of lust. If it is gossip, call it the sin of gossip. If it is selfishness, call it the sin of selfishness.

An old evangelist friend of mine used to say, "God works in the open - Satan works in the hidden." Don't keep your sins hidden but bring them out into the light. Notice what the apostle John said, *If we say that we have fellowship with Him, and walk in darkness, we lie and do not practice the truth. But if we walk in the light as He is in the light, we have fellowship with one another, and the blood of Jesus Christ His Son cleanses us from all sin (1 John 1:6-7, emphasis added).* As another saint of God used to say, "The blood can't cleanse what doesn't come to the light." (Derek Prince)

Confession does not mean that we gloss over or excuse our bad behavior. There must be a realistic recognition of what our sin truly is. It is evil and is contrary to the will of God. Sin is what has caused untold human suffering throughout the ages and sinful patterns keep us from walking in our destiny and fulfilling God's plan for our life. Another way to look at it is that sin is doing anything that Jesus would not do.

Hidden Sins

One major problem is that we don't see our sin. We can't confess what we don't see. Many of our sins remain hidden from us. What if I told you that there is something you are doing that will shorten your life? What if I said that it could weaken your skeletal system and subject you to various bone maladies such as arthritis and osteoporosis – that it would wreak havoc on your immune system making you more susceptible to serious diseases? If you knew I was quoting a trustworthy source wouldn't you want to know what that one thing is?

The Bible plainly teaches that there are ramifications for disobeying the clear commands of God. For example, one of the Ten Commandments is to honor our father and mother. It is repeated again in the New Testament in Ephesians 6:1-3 where Paul instructs us with these words, *Children, obey your parents in the Lord, for this is right. "Honor your father and mother," which is the first commandment with promise: "that it may be well with you and you may live long on the earth."* The implication is that if we break this command things won't go well with us and we won't live out the full allotment of our days on earth. Was there ever a time in your life when you dishonored your parents? Most people have but they don't think to confess and repent of that sin because it remains hidden.

The Japanese enjoy a longer life expectancy than most other people groups including Americans. This may, as some nutritionists point out, be the result of a better diet, or, as someone said to me recently, it may be the result of their culture – a culture of honor where they bestow great honor on their parents. You see it doesn't matter about your culture or your religion or your socio-economic status; when you keep one of God's laws there will be benefit.

Another hidden sin is covetousness. Jesus said, *"Take heed and beware of covetousness. For a man's life consists not in the abundance of the things he possesses"* (Luke 12:15). Jesus is saying, "Take special notice of this one. Why do we have to take heed? Take heed means to be on guard, to watch out. Take heed and beware because this one will sneak up on you and covetousness will open a person up to a host of tormenting problems.

In another place the New International Version translates the word "covetousness" as "selfish desire" and I think that is a very good definition. I believe that covetousness is inseparable from envy and jealousy and are closely tied together in meaning. Some health problems can be traced to the spiritual root of envy/jealousy. *A sound heart is life to the body, but **envy** is rottenness to the bones* (Proverbs 14:30). The immune system has its origin in the bone marrow and envy/jealousy will weaken your body's ability to fight off disease. Scripture teaches that you will live longer if you avoid covetousness (a form of envy/jealousy). *But he who hates covetousness (selfish desire) will prolong his days (Proverbs 28:16b).*

Covetousness will cause you to miss out on your spiritual inheritance. *For this you know, that no fornicator, unclean person, nor covetous man, who is an idolater, has any inheritance in the kingdom of Christ and God* (Ephesians 5:5). God has great blessings in store for His children but envy/jealousy/covetousness will keep us from receiving.

In addition, envy and self-seeking may bring confusion. *But if you have bitter envy and self-seeking in your hearts, do not boast and lie against the truth. This wisdom does not descend from above, but is earthly, sensual, demonic. For where envy and self-seeking exist, confusion and every evil thing are there* (James 3:14-16). Do you have confusion in your life? Look for envy/jealousy/covetousness.

In Luke 12:13-21 a man from the crowd said to Jesus, *Teacher, tell my brother to divide the inheritance with me.* When the last remaining parent dies it amazes me how these nice, loving, thoughtful surviving children suddenly turn postal with one another. They will lie, steal, cheat, malign, and backstab to get what they believe is their rightful share. Isn't that sad?

In Bible days the Mosaic Law said that the oldest son was to receive a double portion of the inheritance. So if a man had seven sons, at his death, his possessions would be divided up into eight equal shares. Each son would receive one-eighth except the oldest who would receive two-eighths – a double portion. So the man in this Gospel story was apparently miffed because his older brother got twice as much, to which Jesus responds, "Take heed and beware of greed" or, as I said, the NIV translates this same word as "selfish desire" in another place.

I received a license to preach, marry and bury way back in 1971 when I became associate pastor of a Baptist Church in California.

Trap Number One: Hidden Sins

In all these years of ministry hundreds and hundreds of people have come to me for counsel. In all these years never has one person approached me because they saw envy/covetousness in their life and wanted freedom. Not until one day, back in 2003, a lady set an appointment to meet with me for prayer ministry. As we began our session I asked her why we needed to meet. She said it was because she wanted freedom from envy. I almost fell out of my chair when she said that. I stood up, shook her hand, and congratulated her on being the first to ever request ministry for that reason.

Even though it wreaks so much havoc in our lives, the tragic truth is that few people recognize when they walk in the spirit of envy/jealousy/covetousness or any other secret sin such as pride and self-pity. I suppose it is rare for us to acknowledge these hidden sins, in part, due to the fact that we are ashamed to admit when they are operating in us. These sins seem so petty and childish when brought out into the open so we tend to play them down or try to ignore them. But God thinks it is so important to deal with covetousness that He made one of His Ten Commandments address the subject. "You shall not covet."

Since so much is at stake, it behooves us to investigate the dynamics of this sin. In Hebrews 13:5-6 we read, *Let your conduct be without covetousness; be content with such things as you have. For He Himself has said, "I will never leave you nor forsake you." So we may boldly say: "The LORD is my helper; I will not fear. What can man do to me?"*

Colossians 3:5. *Therefore put to death your members which are on the earth: fornication, uncleanness, passion, evil desire, and covetousness, which is idolatry.*

Notice that, according to this verse, covetousness is idolatry. So actually when we break this commandment we break another one simultaneously – because we are violating the command that says, "You shall have no other gods before me." In light of the fact that God says so much about this sin it remains hidden from most people.

Other hidden sins include the lack of compassion, lack of humility, lack of gentleness, and lack of patience. *Therefore, as God's chosen people, holy and dearly loved, clothe yourselves with compassion, kindness, humility, gentleness and patience. Bear with each other and forgive whatever grievances you may have against one another. Forgive as the Lord forgave you. And over all these virtues put on love, which binds them all together in perfect unity* (Col. 3:12-14).

Stephen Covey tells of an unusual experience on the New York subway. While people were sitting quietly in the subway car, a man entered with his noisy and rambunctious children. The man sat down and closed his eyes as though he was unaware of his rowdy children. The once quiet subway car was now a disturbing place of chaos. The children's inappropriate behavior was obvious to everyone except their father. Finally, Covey confronted the man about his children. The man opened his eyes and evaluated the situation as if he were unaware of all that had transpired: "Oh, you're right. I guess I should do something about it. We just came from the hospital, where their mother died about an hour ago. I don't know what to think, and I guess they don't know how to handle it either." Compassion starts when we begin to understand the hurts of others.[1] Have you ever lacked compassion, humility, gentleness or patience in regards to another person? Did you ever confess these as sin?

A condemnatory and judgmental heart also grieves the Spirit of God. A man was awakened in the middle of the night by a phone call. On the other end a frantic, sobbing girl managed to get out the words, "Daddy, I'm pregnant." He was groggy and stunned but communicated his forgiveness and prayed with her. The next day he and his wife wrote their daughter two letters of counsel and love. Three days later the man received another phone call. His daughter was shocked by the letters, because she was not the one who had called.

Some other distraught girl had dialed a wrong number. Nonetheless, the letters were not wasted. Their expressions of unconditional love and forgiveness are now a treasured possession. Here are a few excerpts: "Though I weep inside, I can't condemn you, because I sin too. Your transgression is no worse than mine. It's just different. It all comes from the same sin package you inherited through us. We're praying much. We love you more than I can say. And respect you, too, as always. Remember, God's love is in even this, maybe especially in this. This is a day of testing, but hold our ground we must. God will give us the victory. We're looking forward to your being at home. Love, Dad."[2]

Love is the most important moral quality in the believer's life, for it is the very glue that produces unity in the church. Do you ever have a hard time loving someone? Speak to the Holy Spirit who lives in you. Say this, "Holy Spirit, the ability to love is in You, the one who lives in me. I release Your love through me now. Thank you Holy Spirit." For that matter, you can deal thusly with any temptation or sin you're struggling with. The Holy Spirit is our helper and He loves to help us live the victorious Christian life.

Keep in mind that freedom begins with recognition. Recognition is 90% of the solution because if we don't see our sin the way God sees it how can we confess it? Confession means "to say the same thing" that God says about it. But then what do we do after we have confessed and repented and yet we find ourselves doing the same thing over and over? Hang in there with me for the rest of this teaching because I'm convinced that you will gain a new level of freedom.

Another huge problem is that we tend to blame others for our sins. In the Garden of Eden Adam and Eve were given one simple command- Don't eat of the Tree of the Knowledge of Good and Evil. They disobeyed but they didn't own the responsibility. Take a look at this passage. *And they heard the sound of the LORD God walking in the garden in the cool of the day, and Adam and his wife hid themselves from the presence of the LORD God among the trees of the garden. Then the LORD God called to Adam and said to him, "Where are you?"*

When God called for Adam He wasn't just asking for information. He was giving Adam an opportunity to take responsibility and to repent and be restored into fellowship with Him. So he said, "I heard Your voice in the garden, and I was afraid because I was naked; and I hid myself." And He said, "Who told you that you were naked? Have you eaten from the tree of which I commanded you that you should not eat?" Then the man said, "The woman whom You gave to be with me, she gave me of the tree, and I ate." When Adam blamed the woman he was, at the same time, blaming God. And the LORD God said to the woman, "What is this you have done?" The woman said, "The serpent deceived me, and I ate" (Genesis 3:8-13).

Someone once jokingly said, "Adam blamed Eve, Eve blamed the devil, and the devil didn't have a leg to stand on. All kidding aside, this story aptly portrays the tendency of the human race to blame others instead of owning our responsibility in the matter. It does no good to blame your parents for your poor upbringing or blame your teachers for treating you unjustly or blame your spouse for pushing you over the brink. Andy Stanley says it well, "Your best bet for success in the future is to own your part in the past." He also says, "You can't blame your way into a better future." If we want to walk in freedom we have to take responsibility for our part in what we did wrong.

It shouldn't be so hard to simply admit to God and others, "I was wrong." Yet, sometimes those words seem to be the hardest words in the English language to say, but, they are some of the most freeing words.

Confession, though, by itself is not sufficient for your freedom. Another dynamic concerning sin is the necessity of true repentance. The Holy Spirit loaded the Bible with many references to repentance. Jesus taught the people to repent. *From that time Jesus began to preach and to say,* "**Repent***, for the kingdom of* *heaven is at hand"* (Matt. 4:17, emphasis added).

The apostle Paul said, *For godly sorrow produces* **repentance** *leading to salvation, not to be regretted; but the sorrow of the world produces death* (2 Cor. 7:10, emphasis added). We don't want to go around constantly feeling sorrow, guilt and remorse for the bad things we have done. That only produces death. We want the kind of repentance that leads to freedom.

The word repentance in the Greek, the original language of the New Testament, is the word *metanoia* which is made up of two words. "*Meta*" which means "with" and "*noia*" which means "thought." Hence, repentance means that after putting some thought into it, we have a change of mind. We have a change of mind about going our own way and we decide to go God's way, fully turning to God without reservation or excuse.

Sometimes people feel extreme sorrow over their sinful deeds. After the Holy Spirit examines their heart, however, they understand that the sorrow they felt was because they got caught and are afraid they might lose something. There is no mourning over the hurt they have caused.

In the book of 1 Samuel, chapter 15, we find the story of a king who demonstrates false repentance. King Saul was given a command of God, through the prophet Samuel, to go and utterly destroy the Amalekites. He was commanded to kill all the men, women, children and even the animals. These instructions seem extremely harsh as we read this story but we must keep some facts in mind to see it from God's perspective.

The Amalekites were a totally debauched group of people. Not only were they bent on destroying Israel but they often lived as Nomads going out in marauding bands to pillage and obliterate villages of innocent people in order to sustain themselves and to gain wealth. They demonstrated perversion, having sex with their animals so that even their livestock became demonized. God gave them hundreds of years to repent but to no avail. Finally God said,

"Enough is enough, it's time for judgment." God chose Saul to be His instrument to bring His justice to bear on a people group that had, without restraint, brought injustice and suffering into the lives of countless thousands.

King Saul engaged the Amalekites and handily defeated them. When the prophet Samuel showed up on the scene Saul ran out to greet him and enthusiastically saying, "I have performed the commandment of the LORD." And Samuel answered, "Oh, really, then what are those noises I'm hearing? It sounds like the bleating of sheep and the lowing of cattle." (My paraphrase).

The truth is, Saul did obey the command of the Lord, but only partially. Partial obedience is still disobedience. You see he kept some of the best cattle and sheep alive for his own use. Then he blamed the people for his action. He said, ...for the people spared the best of the sheep and the oxen, to sacrifice to the LORD your God (I Sam. 15:15). To fully repent you must accept personal responsibility for what you have done. You cannot hide behind some other person's sinful behavior such as a mom, dad, spouse, or sibling. You can't even blame the devil for your sin. If you sinned, you are responsible for your actions.

In addition, king Saul kept the king of the Amalekites alive. In those days when kings went to war the victor would often keep the defeated king alive and use him as sort of a trophy. Saul received a clear command of the Lord, but after defeating the Amalekites, the wheels began to turn. He thought to himself, "What a waste to simply execute Agag, the king of the Amalekites. I can parade him around in front of the troops and the other people. In doing so it will be a great morale builder." He kept some of the best sheep and cows alive probably because he reasoned that it would be a waste to just kill them. Our human reasoning will get us into trouble because we stop listening to the Lord. God has His reasons and His plans are always best. For whatever reason, when we disobey God we sin.

Keep in mind that I'm not saying these things to bring condemnation and shame to you. I'm simply showing you that un-confessed, un-repented of sin provides and open door for Satan's kingdom to come and oppress and torment you. Dealing with sin is the first giant step toward walking in the freedom God intended for you.

Here is a list of common sins. Go over the list and check off any you have not thoroughly dealt with in genuine repentance. Let the Holy Spirit guide you and try to be as open and honest as you can. The more open and honest you are today, the more you will get out of this seminar.

It is important that we confess specifically the sins we've committed. Just saying, "God, forgive me of all my sins, amen," usually doesn't work. When you sinned, you didn't sin in a general sense, you sinned in a specific sense so this list will help you be specific.

My prayer is that God will open your eyes to see, not to bring you into condemnation, but to enable you to simply confess in order to close this door to the enemy's inroad into your life. However, don't indulge in a naval-gazing self-analysis but simply worship our great God and allow the Holy Spirit to bring to the surface any specific sins you need to deal with. If you are humble and genuinely seeking Him, He will show you. There are two identical pages of common sins, one to fill out now and the other to keep in your syllabus for future use.

Common Sins Worksheet

- ❏ lust
- ❏ impatience
- ❏ desire for revenge
- ❏ cheating
- ❏ passivity
- ❏ outbursts of anger
- ❏ fornication
- ❏ not honoring all people
- ❏ stealing
- ❏ believing Satan's lies about yourself
- ❏ workaholic
- ❏ giving into shame
- ❏ stinginess
- ❏ fear of man
- ❏ addicted to drugs
- ❏ manipulation
- ❏ sexual fantasy
- ❏ complaining
- ❏ disobedience to God
- ❏ compulsive masturbation
- ❏ boastful
- ❏ make fun of people
- ❏ prejudice

- ❏ greed
- ❏ covetousness
- ❏ lying
- ❏ easily offended
- ❏ gossip
- ❏ adultery
- ❏ wandering eye
- ❏ pride
- ❏ sloth
- ❏ judgmental
- ❏ drunkenness
- ❏ worry wart
- ❏ self-centeredness
- ❏ rebellion
- ❏ occultism
- ❏ controlling
- ❏ swearing
- ❏ unbelief
- ❏ pornography
- ❏ idolatry
- ❏ contentious
- ❏ prayerlessness
- ❏ rudeness

Common Sins Worksheet
(Page 2)

- ❏ vanity
- ❏ peeping tom
- ❏ compromise your convictions
- ❏ procrastination
- ❏ distrustful
- ❏ suspicion
- ❏ suppresses ministers and ministries
- ❏ followed false teachers

- ❏ exchange of funds done in ungodly ways
- ❏ illegal substance trafficking

- ❏ trusting in money above trusting in God
- ❏ manipulating, abusing, or oppressing the poor
- ❏ accepting or giving bribes

- ❏ entitlement spirit
- ❏ dishonoring parents
- ❏ seek legitimacy through the approval of people rather than God

- ❏ self-righteous
- ❏ religious spirit
- ❏ irresponsibility

- ❏ jealousy
- ❏ cursing
- ❏ self pity
- ❏ rationalizes the Word

- ❏ contributed to a church split
- ❏ not tithing

- ❏ unpaid earned wages (James 5:4)
- ❏ not caring for the poor

- ❏ materialism

- ❏ not being submissive to God's timing
- ❏ negativity
- ❏ constant criticism

Common Sins Worksheet

- ❏ lust
- ❏ impatience
- ❏ desire for revenge
- ❏ cheating
- ❏ passivity
- ❏ outbursts of anger
- ❏ fornication
- ❏ not honoring all people
- ❏ stealing
- ❏ believing Satan's lies about yourself
- ❏ workaholic
- ❏ giving into shame
- ❏ stinginess
- ❏ fear of man
- ❏ addicted to drugs
- ❏ manipulation
- ❏ sexual fantasy
- ❏ complaining
- ❏ disobedience to God
- ❏ compulsive masturbation
- ❏ boastful
- ❏ make fun of people
- ❏ prejudice
- ❏ greed
- ❏ covetousness
- ❏ lying
- ❏ easily offended
- ❏ gossip
- ❏ adultery
- ❏ wandering eye
- ❏ pride
- ❏ sloth
- ❏ judgmental
- ❏ drunkenness
- ❏ worry wart
- ❏ self-centeredness
- ❏ rebellion
- ❏ occultism
- ❏ controlling
- ❏ swearing
- ❏ unbelief
- ❏ pornography
- ❏ idolatry
- ❏ contentious
- ❏ prayerlessness
- ❏ rudeness

Common Sins Worksheet
(Page 2)

- ❏ vanity
- ❏ peeping tom
- ❏ compromise your convictions
- ❏ procrastination
- ❏ distrustful
- ❏ suspicion
- ❏ suppresses ministers and ministries
- ❏ followed false teachers

- ❏ exchange of funds done in ungodly ways
- ❏ illegal substance trafficking

- ❏ trusting in money above trusting in God
- ❏ manipulating, abusing, or oppressing the poor
- ❏ accepting or giving bribes

- ❏ entitlement spirit
- ❏ dishonoring parents
- ❏ seek legitimacy through the approval of people rather than God

- ❏ self-righteous
- ❏ religious spirit
- ❏ irresponsibility

- ❏ jealousy
- ❏ cursing
- ❏ self pity
- ❏ rationalizes the Word

- ❏ contributed to a church split
- ❏ not tithing

- ❏ unpaid earned wages (James 5:4)
- ❏ not caring for the poor
- ❏ materialism

- ❏ not being submissive to God's timing
- ❏ negativity
- ❏ constant criticism

Once you have completed the Common Sins Worksheet tear it out of your syllabus and hold it in your hands. Let's repeat the following prayer together after me. "Heavenly Father, I acknowledge that I have committed these sins that I checked off. I agree with You that these sins are wicked, ungodly, and against You. Because of these sins I rightfully deserve death on a cross, but I thank You Lord Jesus that You died in my place. By Your grace I turn away from these sins and, instead, I choose to walk in Your ways. With Your help I am dead to these sins and I receive Your full forgiveness and cleansing, in Jesus' Name."

In Colossians 2:13-14 we read, *And you, being dead in your trespasses and the uncircumcision of your flesh, He has made alive together with Him, having forgiven you all trespasses, having wiped out the handwriting of requirements that was against us, which was contrary to us. And He has taken it out of the way, having nailed it to the cross.* Jesus died for our sins 2000 years ago when He hung on the cross but we didn't receive forgiveness automatically - we must adopt by faith what Jesus has already provided. With this truth in mind we're going to do a symbolic act.

Now bring your Common Sins sheet to the front and nail (with a tack pin) them to this wooden cross. Please don't enter into conversation with those around you because this is a very solemn event and you could distract others. As you do this exercise, imagine that your sins are being decisively dealt with by Jesus Christ. After you "nail" your sins to the cross please be seated with your head bowed and eyes close and remain in prayer. (For those not in attendance at an Encounter, who are reading the book, you may improvise at this time. Tack or tape your list of sins to a cross or drawing of a cross as a visual to aid you in letting go of the guilt.)

The leader says, "Now look at me in the eyes while I make some declarations over you. The Bible says that the eyes are the window to the soul and I want to speak to your innermost being."

The leader continues, "I declare that, based on the authority of

God's Word, you are forgiven. I declare that you are not guilty. It is just as if you had never committed these sins one time in your entire life. You are totally forgiven. God promises to remove our sins as far as the east is from the west. You are forgiven in Jesus' Name. As of right now God has forgotten that you ever committed these sins. Now as a man of God and a representative of the Body of Christ, I forgive you."

"When we sin we sometimes allow shame to come upon us and the shame makes us miserable. Therefore, in the Name of Jesus and by the power of His shed blood, I declare that all shame is broken off you right now. I declare that you are not defined by the sins you have committed. You are defined by what God says about you and He says, 'Though your sins be as scarlet they shall be as white as snow.' I break shame off of you, in Jesus' mighty Name."

"No matter what you have done, if you confess and repent forgiveness is yours, in Jesus Christ's Holy Name. There is no sin that is so grotesque that the blood of Jesus cannot wash it away, so I declare that all guilt is broken off you right now, in Jesus' Name. I declare that all condemnation for anything you've done or didn't do is broken off you now, in Jesus' Name. I declare that, based on Romans 8:1, which says, *There is therefore now no condemnation for those who are in Christ*, you are free from condemnation. You are not defined by what you have done because you are a new creation in Christ. I declare that you are cleansed from all condemnation, false guilt, and shame, in Jesus' Name."

"Isaiah 61:1 says this, *The Spirit of the Lord God is upon me because He has anointed me to preach good tidings unto the meek. He has sent me to bind up the broken hearted, to proclaim liberty to the captives and the opening of the prison to them that are bound*. Based on this Scripture I declare over you liberty to the captives. I proclaim the opening of the prison to them that are bound. You are loosed from the prison of shame, guilt and condemnation. You no longer have to serve prison time. You no longer have to serve punishment time for the things you have done or left undone because Jesus took all of your punishment when He suffered on the cross. I declare these truths over you, in Jesus' powerful Name."

Your Declaration

Say these words after me out loud.

"I am a new creation in Christ Jesus. I am forgiven and cleansed by His blood. The old me has passed away and all things have become new. Jesus lives in me and greater is He who is in me than he who is in the world. My heavenly Father loves me with a perfect, unfailing love. I am loved. I am kept by His blood. I am accepted. I am not a victim. I am an over comer through Him who loves me. The very same Spirit that raised Jesus from the dead, lives in me, in Jesus' Name." (Now spend some time praising, thanking and worshipping God.)

CHAPTER THREE
Trap Number Two: Unforgiveness

The number one reason people don't get free is they don't forgive. See Matt. 6:14-15. *For if you forgive men their trespasses, your heavenly Father will also forgive you. But if you do not forgive men their trespasses, neither will your Father forgive your trespasses.*

Unforgiveness/forgiveness is mentioned 120 times in the Bible. It's a huge issue. God wants us to know that without forgiveness there will be no freedom.

Matthew 18 is the only parable where Jesus gave an unsolicited explanation of the parable. That parable speaks of a steward that owed the king 10,000 talents. A talent was a measure of precious metal. In today's economy that would be the equivalent of about 60 million dollars! That represented an unpayable debt for a servant working at minimum wage. If he saved every cent he earned he would not be able to pay off the debt in his lifetime.

In those days they had severe ways of dealing with people who couldn't pay their debts. One method was to sell them into slavery along with their wife and children. The king threatened to do so and the steward panicked as most of us would do if we were in his shoes. The servant begged the king for mercy and, to his amazement, the king had pity on him and forgave him of that entire debt. The steward went his way and found a fellow servant who owed him 100 denari. A denarius was approximately worth a day's wage. In today's economy that is approximately $80.00. So 100 denari was still a good chunk of change but it was a payable debt.

The fellow servant didn't have the means to pay so the steward threw him in prison. In those days a debtors prison was more horrific than just being thrown into a dark dungeon. Not only was the debtor incarcerated but he was tortured. The idea was that because of the ongoing torture the extended family and friends would feel sorry for him and work to pool their resources to pay off the debt.

The steward's fellow servants found out about what he did and went and told the king. The king was furious. So he called in the steward and said, "I forgave you of that entire debt and you wouldn't forgive your fellow servant of a hundred denari?" So he had that steward thrown into prison and he turned him over to the tormentors or torturers.

Then Jesus ends that parable by saying, *So shall My Heavenly Father do to you if you don't forgive your brother from your heart.* That closing statement contains some powerful truths that we need to think about. It says God will turn us over to the tormentors. I believe this is not a matter of going to the Lake of Fire when we die but rather it is something that happens to us right now in this life. When we refuse to forgive it opens the door for the enemy to come in and torment our lives. We become miserable, bitter and angry.

The Greek word for forgiveness is *aphiemi* which literally means "to remit a punishment or cancel a debt." When a person hurts us we feel they owe us something. To forgive, we need to cancel the debt. Imagine yourself in the place of the steward in Jesus' parable. He had just been forgiven of an unpayable debt but refused to forgive the debt of his fellow servant. It's like us. When we trust in Christ for salvation God forgives us of our unpayable debt and cancels the sin of our rebellion towards Him. Likewise, we need to cancel the debts of those we feel owe us.

At times we may not want to forgive because we think if we forgive the person who hurt us they will get off scot free. The truth is that it's like I'm drinking a bottle of poison and hoping it hurts my offender. Our bitterness hurts us far more than it hurts them. God is able to mete out vengeance if that is His will. "Vengeance is mine, I will repay says the LORD." If there is any vengeance that's God's business. We need to take our hands completely off the need to make the person suffer for what they did. Sometimes we think that if I give up my resentments I will have nothing left to defend myself but why can't we trust God to defend us? The Bible says, *It is better to trust in the LORD than to put confidence in man* (Psalm 118:8).

When we forgive it frees God to deal with that person. Ruby (not her real name) had a major screaming match with her mother stemming from mom's manipulative techniques. For many years her mother refused to talk to her in spite of Ruby's many efforts to break the ice. Through the help of a prayer minister at church Ruby forgave her mother from her heart. Her mother called her within days to reconcile. Often positive things happen spiritually in the life of the other person when we choose to forgive.

The other thing that Jesus teaches in this parable is that we must forgive from the heart. Most Christians know that we must forgive but the forgiveness given is usually only at the head level. That's a good place to start but we must go further and forgive down deep, at the heart level. Bitterness left in the heart will come out in one way or another but, make no mistake, it will come out. Often bitterness/unforgiveness manifests itself in various physical ailments, arthritis and heart disease to name a few. The apostle Paul said, *Be angry and sin not. Let not the sun go down on your wrath, neither give place to the devil* (Eph. 4:26-27). The word for "place" in this verse is the Greek word *topos*, from which we get our English word "topography." We literally give the devil a piece of real estate in our lives when we let anger and bitterness fester by not dealing with it.

Another major problem that unforgiveness causes is it hinders our prayer life. Notice that right after the teaching on the Lord's Prayer, in the context of prayer, Jesus talks about the danger of unforgiveness. In Mark chapter 11, Jesus is teaching on prayer and watch what He says, *And whenever you stand praying, if you have anything against anyone, forgive him, that your Father in heaven may also forgive you your trespasses. But if you do not forgive, neither will your Father in heaven forgive your trespasses* (vv. 25-26).

One Sunday I preached a sermon on prayer. After the service a faithful church member said to me, "Pastor, I used to have a powerful prayer life. I enjoyed spending much time in fervent, believing prayer but lately my ability to connect with God in prayer is gone. I have no real desire to pray and when I do it's just like I'm going through the motions." I looked at her and I said, "Anita (not her real name), you have unforgiveness in your heart." She said emphatically, "I do not!" I said, "Yes you do." She was starting to take offense so I said, "I can almost guarantee it but just in case, will you go home and ask God if you are harboring any unforgiveness?" She agreed to do so.

The next Sunday she approached me with a beaming smile and her face lit up. With great enthusiasm she said, "Pastor, you were right. God showed me some unforgiveness and I didn't even know it was there. I confessed it and now my prayer life is back. It worked, it worked! Thank you Pastor."

How often should we forgive? Fortunately the Bible answers that question. Then Peter came to Him and said, *"Lord, how often shall my brother sin against me, and I forgive him? Up to seven times?" Jesus said to him, "I do not say to you, up to seven times, but up to seventy times seven"* (Matthew 18:21-22).

Trap Number Two: Unforgiveness

In his heart I'm sure Peter thought he was being magnanimous when he suggested seven times. Instead Jesus said, "No seventy times seven" which equals 490 times. Does this mean that we may add up the offences a person commits against us and when the number surpasses 490 we have the right to clobber them? No. Jesus is saying that we never stop forgiving. Aren't you glad that our Heavenly Father doesn't stop forgiving us after 490 times? Most of us would be in serious trouble.

However, it's important to know that just because I forgive a person doesn't mean I trust them. For example, if I was molested by my uncle as a child I must forgive him but that doesn't mean that I would trust him to babysit my kids. Trust and forgiveness are two different things. Forgiveness is given, trust is earned. If you got caught stealing money from the church offering plate I wouldn't trust you to be the church treasurer. In fact, it would be downright stupid, unless there had been true repentance and restitution and a sufficient period of time had transpired for you prove yourself trustworthy.

Forgiveness does not mean that I let the person violate my boundaries. Every person needs clearly defined boundaries lest others take unfair advantage. Don't let yourself be manipulated or used in the name of forgiveness. We can forgive and still keep our boundaries in place.

Forgiveness also does not mean that you have been healed of the wounding the other person caused. You may have genuinely forgiven but your heart needs to be mended because what they did hurt so badly. In such cases I suggest that you put your hand on your heart and ask the Lord to pull up the pain and heal your heart. He said He came to heal the broken hearted and that includes your heart.

How do you know whether or not you have truly forgiven from your heart a person I'll call Bob? When you think of him do strong emotions well up inside you? If you see him in church or at the grocery store do you try to avoid him? When bad things happen to him do you silently rejoice? Do you contemplate ways of getting revenge? You know the Bible says to, *Bless those who persecute you; bless and curse not*, but you can't sincerely bless Bob. If you have unforgiveness towards Bob, every time his name comes up, every time you think about him, he yanks your chain. (show picture of a chain on the screen). But the minute you forgive that chain is cut and freedom comes.

Often people don't want to forgive because they think they must excuse the offense, that the perpetrator was not wrong or that he is not accountable to anyone. The truth is that when we forgive, we leave room for the culprit to be held liable. *Do not take revenge, my dear friends, but leave room for God's wrath, for it is written: "It is mine to avenge; I will repay," says the Lord.* (Romans 12:19, NIV). When we let go of the offense it frees God to move to bring about justice.

Sometimes it really helps to keep in mind that "Hurt people hurt people" and that "Sick people infect people." People wound us out of their own wounding. As a teenager my cousin Jim (not his real name) took a trip with his parents to Wisconsin to visit a great aunt he had never seen. They had a cute little dog that seemed friendly enough so he patted it on the head and scratched it behind the ears. The dog was eating up the affection so Jim, knowing that most dogs love to have you scratch their belly, reached underneath the dog and started scratching. The good natured pet suddenly turned vicious and bit Jim on the face taking a huge chunk out of his upper lip. The dog was a nice pet, but, unknown to Jim, it had a big sore on its belly. Out of its woundedness it lashed out at someone seeking it no harm. The wound on Jim's lip healed but left an ugly scar. As an adult Jim always wears a mustache to cover his lip. This illustrates what happens in human relationships. People hurt others because they themselves are wounded.

A lot of Christians think that if they forgive they have to forget. But nowhere in the Bible does it say we must forget. It also doesn't mean that we can't feel angry but people often deny their anger.

Trap Number Two: Unforgiveness

Unfortunately, the anger will come out in some way whether it be by their behavior or health issues. In the Psalms David owned his anger and frustration and he poured out his complaint to God. If you are angry, own up to your anger and express it. Forgiveness is not the termination of anger. It is a matter of faith letting go of the offense and bringing it to the Cross for Christ to deal with. We need to let God know when something makes us angry or frustrated, but do not hold on to it, give it to the Lord and express the anger or frustration to Him and ask Him to help you release it to His care. Eventually the anger will vanish away as the Cross does its work.

Today we're going to forgive the three hardest people for us to forgive, the three that hurt us the most. If it was a church or an organization it's okay to lump them together rather than naming individually every single person in that group. Keep in mind that, even though you have truly forgiven you may continue to hurt because of their actions. We will deal with the hurt later on when we teach on trauma.

Please stand and close your eyes and pray corporately, "Lord Jesus, who do I need to forgive? Now Lord bring them to my mind right now. The person that hurt me, disappointed me, the person I need to forgive."

Listen and wait for the Lord to bring that person to your mind.

"Now Lord, play the video in their mind. I ask You to show them anyone that they need to forgive today. Lord, if there's someone who abused them, betrayed them, did horrible things to them, right now Lord, I ask you to do this great thing."

Keep your eyes closed and let the Lord show you this thing and as He shows you who you need to forgive, put your hand up to your mouth and whisper in your hand this prayer.

Repeat this prayer after me: "Father I forgive _____ for all he/she did to me. I'm not keeping score. They owe me nothing. I let them go free. I forgive them fully from my heart because

You always forgive me. Now I ask you to bless them in every way, financially, spiritually, in their relationships and in their health (See Matt. 5:44)."

Say, "Lord, I choose to forgive _____. " Picture yourself with a stack of I.O.U's with that person's name on them. Each I.O.U represents what you feel that person owes you. Now take that stack and tear those notes up and throw them on the ground, representing that you are releasing them from the debt. Then reach up and give the unforgiveness to the Lord. The Lord wants you to leave here free so say, "Lord I choose to forgive."

Now when you feel a peace or release and you sense that you have truly forgiven that person you may be seated. Don't sit down until you know in your heart that you have released that person. If you can't get a breakthrough one of the team members will come and pray for you individually. If you are reading this book you may do these exercises on your own but it is helpful to get someone to pray with you.

(In the Encounter seminar the leader repeats this process two more times.)

If you feel that you have more people to forgive we're going to ask the Lord to bring the second hardest person to your mind. Please stand and repeat after me. "Lord Jesus, who is the next person You want me to forgive? Lord bring them to my mind right now."

"Now Lord, play the video in their mind. I ask You Lord to show them the number two person that they need to forgive today. Lord, if there's someone who abused them, betrayed them, did horrible things to them, lied about them, stole from them, right now Lord, I ask you to do this great thing."

Keep your eyes closed and let the Lord show you this thing and as He shows you who you need to forgive, put your hand up to your mouth and whisper in your hand this prayer.

Repeat this prayer after me: "Father I forgive _____ for all

Trap Number Two: Unforgiveness

he/she did to me. I'm not keeping score. They owe me nothing. I let them go free. I forgive them fully from my heart because You always forgive me. Now I ask you to bless them in every way, financially, spiritually, in their relationships and in their health (Matt. 5:44)."

Say, "Lord, I choose to forgive _____." Picture yourself with a stack of I.O.U's with that person's name on them. Each I.O.U represents what you feel that person owes you. Now take that stack and tear those notes up and throw them on the ground, representing that you are releasing them from the debt. Then reach up and give that unforgiveness to the Lord. The Lord wants this group to leave here free so say, "Lord I choose to forgive."

Now when you feel a peace or release and you sense that you have truly forgiven that person you may be seated. Don't sit down until you know in your heart that you have released that person. If you can't get a breakthrough one of the team members will come and pray for you individually.

(In the Encounter seminar the leader, repeats this process one more time.)

CHAPTER FOUR

Trap Number Three: Inner Vows and Judgments, Lies, and Expectancies

Most Christians don't know what an inner vow is. Some vows are good vows. The vows I made to my wife on our wedding day were good vows because I made them to her and before God and the assembly. But an inner vow is a vow I make to myself to be carried out by my own power and strength. I get in trouble in my Christian walk when I rely on my own ability. See Jeremiah 17:5, *Thus says the LORD: "Cursed is the man who trusts in man and makes flesh his strength, whose heart departs from the LORD."*

Inner vows are based on judgments. Somebody hurts us or does something we react strongly against and we judge them. Inwardly we vow that we will never do that or will never allow that to happen again to us. Judgments activate the impartial law of sowing and reaping - what we sow is what we reap. If I sow judgment I am going to reap judgment. Jesus said, **Judge** *not that you be not **judged**. For with what judgment you judge, you will be judged; and with the measure you use, it will be measured back to you* (Matt. 7:1-2).

Inner vows don't just go away over time. Some inner vows we may have made in early childhood and we have forgotten that we ever made them, but they put us on a course whereby we continually reap negative consequences. When I see negative fruit that repeatedly manifests in a person's life I know that underneath the bitter fruit there is most likely an inner vow. That vow needs to be broken. The bitter fruit keeps showing up no matter how much effort we expend in trying to change. Inner vows typically begin with the phrase, "I will never." Keep in mind that most inner vows are not even spoken out loud and that is why it is often difficult to locate them on your own.

Inner vows frequently work like a pendulum. For example, let's say that you were raised in a home where your parents struggled financially, living from pay check to pay check, and were often late on paying bills. You hated living under such circumstances so you vowed that when you became an adult you would never struggle financially like your parents. You grow up and you fight to tread water and often get behind on your bills - or the pendulum could swing the opposite direction. You become a workaholic and are never home so that your children grow in an essentially fatherless home. Your wife can't stand the loneliness and she files for divorce. The inner vow gets played out but perhaps not in the same way your parents struggled. Or, let's say dad is an alcoholic. You judge him and make the vow that you'll never be an alcoholic like dad. You grow up and, sure enough, you become an alcoholic. Or, instead, you become what is called a "dry alcoholic" and develop dysfunctions in other areas.

Foundational lies represent another factor that disrupt our lives. People often believe lies that hold them in bondage. The lies I speak of are core lies we believe about God, ourselves and others. The lies about God are things we, as mature Christians, would never believe about God rationally, in our heads. But the problem is that when we experience trauma, especially as children, our hearts become fertile soil for the devil to sow these lies. We don't believe these lies intellectually but the lies are implanted deep in

Trap Number Three: Inner Vows and Judgments, Lies, and Expectancies

our hearts, so when the rubber meets the road, when facing the challenges of everyday life, we act or react according to what is in our heart. We need to locate any such lies and uproot them.

As children what we believe about our earthly father gets transferred to our Heavenly Father. If dad didn't provide for your needs it's easy to believe the lie that "God will not provide." If dad was gone a lot and didn't spend time with you, you may believe the lie that God won't be there for you. If dad didn't mentor you and work with you to guide you in the wise way to manage money then you may believe the lie that "God won't give me the wisdom and guidance in managing my affairs." If dad was a womanizer and this really hurt your mother, you will be tempted to believe the lie that God is not faithful, that God can't be trusted. If dad abandoned the family when you were young the door is opened for the devil to implant the lie that God will abandon you.

The key to freedom is first to recognize these lies. Once we see them and the destruction they have caused we must confess to God our sin in believing them. Then we cast down the structure using our authority in Christ. Say, "Father, I repent for believing the lie that _____. In Jesus' Name, I reject, renounce and break all agreements with this lie." Then ask God what His truth is regarding this lie. Jesus said, *You shall know the truth, and the truth shall make you free* (John 8:32). We need a truth encounter in order to be totally set free from the lie we have believed.

Expectancies work in a similar fashion. For example, you received a lot of rejection as a child. You developed the expectancy that you will be rejected and, sure enough, people reject you wherever you go. Let's say you always went without as a child and eventually you develop an expectancy that you will always go without. An expectancy is the devil's form of faith- you draw "lack" to yourself. You put out vibes that tempt others to underpay you or withhold wages, etc. Or for instance, as a young person you worked hard babysitting and you only got paid a dollar an hour. You work odds jobs to earn some extra money and you get short-changed. Out of these types of experiences you develop an expectancy that you will never get paid what you are worth. And sure enough, you grow up, get different jobs and no matter where you go you don't get paid what you are worth. These expectancies project on other people to respond in a way they would not ordinarily act. Thus, the expectancy gets repeatedly reinforced.

I heard a story about a man who repeatedly lost his job wherever he went. He landed a new job and did very well. He worked hard, was always on time, worked intelligently, a team player, had great ideas and his boss was quite pleased with him. So the boss wanted to give him special recognition for a job well done. He called all of his employees together for the purpose of patting him on the back publically. Then, to his surprise, he commenced raking his new employee over the coals, berating him, and unabashedly shaming him. The other employees looked on not believing their boss would do such a thing. When the meeting was over the boss walked away shaking his head, asking himself, "Why did I do that? That was totally the opposite of what I planned to do."

The truth is that the employee had developed the strong expectations that, "I will displease my authorities," that "The harder I try the more I will fail." Consequently, he continually experienced the responses he hated.

Here is a list of common inner vows, judgments, lies and expectancies that could be active in your life. This is not an exhaustive list but represents the most common ones. Check off any lies you've ever believed, the inner vows you've made and any expectancies you've developed. If God brings others to mind write them down in the space below.

Trap Number Three: Inner Vows and Judgments, Lies, and Expectancies

___ I will never trust my authorities

___ I will never be like dad

___ I will never be like mom

___ I will never marry a man like dad

___ I will never marry a woman like mom

___ I will never be poor

___ I will never go without

___ I will never be lazy

___ I will never trust dad

___ I will never trust authorities

___ I will never let people use me

___ I will never open my heart to others

___ I will never step foot inside a church again

___ No one will listen to me

___ I have no voice

___ My opinion will not matter

___ What I have will be taken from me

___ Those I love will be taken from me

___ My worth is in what I do

___ I'm worthless

___ I will never change

___ I will always suffer lack

___ I will be treated unjustly

Pathway to Freedom

___ I can't share my secrets with mom

___ I can never be good enough

___ I don't fit in

___ My kids will never be poor like I was

___ Women are to be used

___ I'll never have a marriage like my parents

___ I will never be an alcoholic

___ If I drink I will be cool

___ I should have been a boy

___ It's my responsibility to make people happy

___ I'm not lovable

___ I have to be a peace keeper

___ I have to stuff my feelings

___ I will never love again

___ I will be betrayed

___ No one will protect me

___ If I'm invisible I won't be hurt

___ Dad/God will not keep his promises

___ Dad/God won't be there for me

___ Men/women can't be trusted

___ Men/women will use me

___ No one will mentor me

___ I will never be forced to do what I don't want to do

Trap Number Three: Inner Vows and Judgments, Lies, and Expectancies

___ No matter how hard I try I will always struggle financially

_____

_____

_____

PRAYER TO BREAK JUDGEMENTS, INNER VOWS, LIES AND EXPECTANCIES

"Heavenly Father, I confess to you that I have sinned by judging others, myself and You. I turn away from these judgments and by Your grace I am dead to them. I receive Your forgiveness as the blood of Jesus cleanses me now. I also confess my sin of making inner vows and I acknowledge that in making them I was relying on my own strength rather than on You. I confess that I was wrong to have believed lies about You, myself and others and I reject, renounce, and break all agreements with these lies. I also confess the sin of developing ungodly expectancies and I utterly reject them.

"In Jesus' Name, I reject, renounce and break all agreements with the lies, vows and expectancies that _____ (name all that you have checked off on your worksheet.) I break the power of these ungodly lies, vows and expectancies over every aspect of my being, including my relationships, my marriage (or future marriage), my finances, my health, my ministry, my vocation, and my destiny. I decree and declare that these lies, vows, and expectancies are broken, in Jesus' Name."

CHAPTER FIVE

Trap Number Four: Soul Ties and Trauma Bonds

Another trap that the enemy sets for our souls is what we commonly refer to as "Soul Ties." The term is actually a misnomer because the whole person, spirit, soul and body can be tied to another human being, but for our purposes we will refer to it simply as a "soul tie."

What is the Biblical basis for this concept? In 1 Samuel 18:1 we read, *And it came to pass, when he had made an end of speaking unto Saul, that the **soul** of Jonathan was knit with the **soul** of David, and Jonathan loved him as his own **soul**.* Jonathan may have opened the door to an ungodly soul tie with David through his manipulation and control. Manipulation and control will cause the development of an ungodly soul tie.

In the New Testament, in I Corinthians 6:16-17 we read, *Or do you not know that he who is joined to a harlot is **one** body with her? For "the two," He says, "shall become **one** flesh." But he who is joined to the Lord is **one** spirit with Him*. Another way we develop ungodly soul ties is through sexual sin. If a man sleeps with ten women before marrying his wife he has ungodly spirit, soul, and body ties with those women. When he goes to bed with his wife he brings those 10 women to bed with him. His human spirit is searching for those women, thus making it harder for him to form a deep bond with his wife. The same holds true for the wife. If you view pornography and fantasize about those individuals you also build ungodly soul ties with them.

Sometimes a married person will commit "spiritual adultery" with another person. Spiritual adultery happens when you begin to bond spirit to spirit with another person, confiding in them, sharing your secrets, and having lustful thoughts. Spiritual adultery does not entail physical sex but it is a matter of the heart. Spiritual adultery leads to the development of an ungodly soul tie.

I also recommend to all the people I minister to in a private ministry session that they cut the soul ties with any ex-spouses. If a married couple had sex before marriage they have an ungodly soul tie because God forbids premarital sex. In this case we break the ungodly soul tie, but at the same time, we pray for the strengthening of the godly soul tie. It is imperative that we break all ungodly soul ties. The spirit of the husband and wife need to be knit together in a holy way because without this bond you will never experience true intimacy.

I teach couples an exercise to facilitate this bonding process. I tell them to go home and strip down from the waist up and hug each other with their chests touching. At the same time, without words, without expectation that this exercise will lead to sex, communicate from the heart to their spouse. Do this exercise for about 10 minutes at a time and repeat it for two or three days. It will help you bond spirit to spirit.

Another way to form ungodly soul ties is through abuse. If you were abused by someone, they took control over you, thus opening the door for an ungodly soul tie. And it works the other way around. If you abused someone you also formed an ungodly soul tie. Quite often, before you can fully forgive an abuser, you

Trap Number Four: Soul Ties and Trauma Bonds

have to cut the soul tie.

Forming covenants can also build ungodly soul ties. Some of these covenants may have been made in innocence as a child. For example, two friends cut their wrists and put their wrists together, comingling their blood, to form a pact in blood. The problem is that when there is an ungodly covenant, their "stuff" flows to you and your "stuff" to them. The enemy construes the act as legal ground to use against you. No wonder we can't get free from our junk. In addition, covenants with ungodly organizations pose a similar problem

I have often witnessed that when a person goes to a fortune teller, a tarot card reader, a psychic, or shaman, they develop an ungodly soul tie with that person. And it makes it impossible to completely remove occultic influence from their life until they break the soul tie. Soul ties represent a powerful tool in the hands of the enemy.

Not all soul ties are bad. I have a godly soul tie with my wife. The Bible says, And the two shall be one flesh. I am bonded to my wife on a spiritual and physical level. I can also have godly soul ties with my parents or other relatives. That is good and right and proper to have formed a soul tie with them. But when they die, at the appropriate time, after we've had sufficient time to grieve, it proves helpful to cut the soul tie. Doing so will aid in the healing process. After sufficient time to heal I recommend that a woman cut the soul tie with any baby that she miscarried or that died in the birthing process because part of her continues to grieve the loss of the child. Cutting the soul tie enables the mother to release the child into the loving hands of Jesus. Cutting the soul tie with a dead relative, one you were really close to, one whose death caused great trauma in you, will help you to let them go so that you can heal. For adopted children it helps to cut the soul tie with them and their biological parents so they can bond more fully with their adoptive parents.

Sometimes pet owners will subconsciously build a soul tie with a beloved pet because of their emotional attachment. Some people adore their animal to the point of making it an idol. The death of the pet leads to great devastation in the owner and they grieve its loss for months or even years. In this case they must break the soul tie.

Prayer to Break Soul Ties

Please repeat after me and confess any sins that apply. "Heavenly Father, I confess and repent of all sexual sin including ungodly sexual fantasies. I confess and repent of abusing another person in any way. I confess and repent of all manipulation and/or allowing myself to be manipulated. I confess and repent of controlling another person and/or allowing myself to be controlled. I confess and repent of all spiritual adultery. I confess and repent of making any person, animal, or thing an idol."

"Heavenly Father, please break my soul tie with _____ (put your hand in front of your mouth and softly speak their names if you remember. If you don't remember their name describe the person.) Father, please release them from me and release me from them. As I pray this Lord, I ask that you cause them to be all that you want them to be and that you cause me to be all that you want me to be, in Jesus' Name, Amen."

The leader then says, "I take my sword and I sever each and every one of these ungodly soul ties. I pull any of their spirit, soul, and body that doesn't belong there up out of you and send that part back to them. I pull any part of you out of them that doesn't belong there and send it back into you, in Jesus' Name."

Trauma Bonds

I have discovered that, not only can we build a soul tie, which is a direct link to another person, but we can also establish a trauma bond that causes an indirect link to another person or persons. How does this happen? First of all keep in mind that the Bible has a lot to say about the land. For instance, 2 Chronicles 7:14 says, *If My people who are called by My name will humble themselves, and pray and seek My face, and turn from their wicked ways, then I will hear from heaven, and will forgive their sin and heal their **land*** (emphasis added). Another example is found in Psalm 106:38. *And shed innocent blood, The blood of their sons and daughters, Whom they sacrificed to the idols of Canaan; And the **land** was polluted with blood.*

Arthur Burk with Sapphire Ministries teaches that when a person receives severe trauma they can develop a trauma bond to the land where they were traumatized. The trauma bond creates an indirect link with all other people who received trauma on that same piece of property. This indirect link works similarly to a soul tie. All those bonded to a parcel of land through trauma get connected to everyone else who is bonded to that property. I have learned that a person can heal more quickly from past traumatic events by breaking trauma bonds to land.

Remember that the enemy seeks legal ground to establish an opening into our lives. The Lord showed me that when we can't get the devil to leave in a particular area of our lives it's usually because he has some type of legal ground or something that he tries to construe as legal ground. I have found that when we pray to break a trauma bond and it doesn't break, quite often it is because the person shed their blood on that piece of property. In the Bible when a covenant was made between two parties it entailed the shedding of blood. Ultimately, the greatest covenant of all was cut when Jesus shed His blood on Calvary's cross so that we might enter into a covenant relationship with Almighty God. The enemy also understands the importance of covenant and that blood is a vital part of that agreement. He sees the blood a person shed on the land as his legal right to hold the person captive to that land. Consequently, I ask Father to loose His holy angels to go to the land where the accident or abuse occurred and clean up every particle, every molecule, and every subatomic particle of the individual's blood and take it to where Jesus wants it to go. Then I lead the person to pray a prayer telling them to repeat it after me.

Prayer to Break Trauma Bonds

"Heavenly Father, I ask You to break my trauma bond to the land at _____ (provide address or description of where it is located). Release me from that land and release that land from me. As I pray this Lord, I ask that you would release me from any indirect ties I have with those who were traumatized there. I release those people from me and I release myself from those people. I also ask You Father to release those people from any trauma bonds they have to that land. I ask that You would send your angels to clean up any of my blood that may have been spilled on that property and retrieve that blood, down to the subatomic particles and take it where You want it to go. I ask that You would annul any ungodly covenant, in Jesus' Name, Amen." Now wait in faith until you get a peace or release in your spirit that it is done.

CHAPTER SIX

Trap Number Five: Occultic Influence

One reason people can't walk in freedom is because they fail to break with the occult. There are levels of occultism.

1. Flirtation

Ouija Boards, Bloody Mary, Eight Balls, demonic games such as Masters of the Universe, Dungeons and Dragons, Charlie Charlie, Magic: The Gathering and World of WarCraft.

2. Invocation

Where people realize they can get something from occultism and that's a much harder level to deal with. I read a book some years ago on Wicca (witchcraft) by a man who is a former Wiccan. He said something that interested me. I used to think that the reason most people got into witchcraft was for power. That is part of it, but the main reason people get into it is for wisdom. In their PR, Wiccans say that the word "Wicca" means wise, or "wise one." Other people get into occultism to gain greater control.

3. Dedication

People who come out of cults and satanic rituals are the toughest and they take the longest. Many of them were ritually abused as children and programmed to be cult loyal, and some of them are programmed to tear up churches and ministries. Ritually abused people are also DID (Dissociative Identity Disorder). This degree makes it difficult to get them free, but when they get free they get free indeed.

However, a lot of people don't give up their brand of occultism and that's why they don't get free.

How can past occult involvement affect us today?

- All occult involvement wounds. It jolts us; God did not design us for it.
- It disrupts our ability to feel the healthy flow of the Holy Spirit in our lives.
- It creates an inclination toward sin.
- It immediately attracts evil spirits to ensnare us to sin.

What are some effects of occult involvement in families?

- Continuous family disputes and division
- Endless drain on family finances
- Physical illnesses and recurring accidents
- Disrupted sleep
- Mental blockages
- Voices
- Emotional distress

Trap Number Five: Occultic Influence

- Mental illness
- Impediment of destiny
- Demonization
- Propensity toward occult involvement

13 Forbidden Occultic Practices

In the OT God made it clear to the Children of Israel that they were not to copy, imitate or do what the people of Canaan were doing. Likewise, we as the New Testament church are to avoid these practices.

- **Enchantments**, the imparting of magical qualities or effects. *But these two things shall come to you in a moment, in one day: the loss of children, and widowhood. They shall come upon you in their fullness because of the multitude of your sorceries, for the great abundance of your **enchantments*** (Isaiah 47:9).

- **Witchcraft**, practice of using magic or sorcery. *There shall not be found among you anyone who makes his son or his daughter pass through the fire, or one who practices witchcraft, or a soothsayer, or one who interprets omens, or a sorcerer* (Deuteronomy 18:10).

- **Sorcery**, same as witchcraft. *And I will come near you for judgment; I will be a swift witness against **sorcerers**, against adulterers, against perjurers, against those who exploit wage earners and widows and orphans, and against those who turn away an alien—because they do not fear Me, says the LORD of hosts* (Malachi 3:5).

- **Soothsaying**, the practice or art of foretelling events. *For You have forsaken Your people, the house of Jacob, because they are filled with eastern ways; they are **soothsayers** like* *the Philistines, and they are pleased with the children of foreigners* (Isaiah 2:6).

- **Divination**, the practice of attempting to foretell future events or discover hidden knowledge by occult or supernatural means. *You shall not eat anything with the blood, nor shall you practice **divination** or soothsaying* (Leviticus 19:26).

- **Wizardry**, the practicing of magic. A wizard is a male witch and a witch is a female who practices witchcraft. *And when they say to you, "Seek those who are mediums and **wizards**, who whisper and mutter," should not a people seek their God? Should they seek the dead on behalf of the living?"* (Isaiah 8:19).

- **Necromancy**, divination by means of communication with the dead. *There shall not be found among you anyone who makes his son or his daughter pass through the fire, or one who practices witchcraft, or a soothsayer, or one who interprets omens, or a sorcerer, or one who conjures spells, or a medium, or a spiritist, or **one who calls up the dead*** (Deut. 18:10-11).

- **Magic**, the art of producing a desired effect or result through the use of incantation or various other techniques that seem to assure human control of the supernatural or the forces of nature. *Also, many of those who had practiced **magic** brought their books together and burned them in the sight of all and they counted up the value of them, and it totaled fifty thousand pieces of silver* (Acts 19:19).

- **Charms**, any action supposed to have magical power, the chanting or recitation of a magic verse or formula, to put a spell upon. *"The spirit of Egypt will fail in its midst; I will destroy their counsel, and they will consult the idols and the **charmers**, the mediums and the sorcerers. And the Egyptians I will give into the hand of a cruel master, and a* fierce king will rule over them," says the Lord, the LORD of hosts (Isaiah 19:3-4).

- **Prognostication,** the act of forecasting or predicting, to foretell by indications, omens, signs, etc. *You are wearied in the multitude of your counsels; let now the astrologers, the stargazers, and the monthly **prognosticators** stand up and save you from what shall come upon you* (Isaiah 47:13). Current examples include horoscopes, the reading of tea leaves, and tarot cards.

- **Consulting with mediums**. A medium is a person who has fine-tuned his or her extrasensory perception and can tune into the spirits in other dimensions and sense or hear what they are saying. *Also he caused his sons to pass through the fire in the Valley of the Son of Hinnom; he practiced soothsaying, used witchcraft and sorcery, and consulted **mediums** and spiritists. He did much evil in the sight of the LORD, to provoke Him to anger* (2 Chronicles 33:6).

Note: One of the abominable practices of Canaanite worship was the burning of their children in the fire as sacrifices to the god Molech in the Valley of the Son of Hinnom. Molech was an idol made out of cast iron with its belly hollowed out and with its arms stretched out. The people would build a red hot fire in the cavity of the idol and place their newborn babies in its outstretched arms to cook, while they committed sexual orgies.

- **Spiritism**. Spiritists often try and contact the spirits, which can include people who have died in order to learn about the future, to influence the outcome of future events, and to gain knowledge. *Also he caused his sons to pass through the fire in the Valley of the Son of Hinnom; he practiced soothsaying, used witchcraft and sorcery, and consulted mediums and **spiritists**. He did much evil in the sight of the LORD, to provoke Him to anger* (2 Chronicles 33:6).

- **Astrology and star gazing**, divination by stars. *Thus says* *the LORD: "Do not learn the way of the Gentiles; Do not be dismayed at the **signs of heaven**, For the Gentiles are dismayed at them"* (Jeremiah 10:2). What is the difference between astronomy and occultism? Astronomy is science, it studies the movements of planets and stars, their size and shape, etc. Astrology is spiritual, it is a form of occultism and appears to be light but it is a counterfeit of the true Light of God.

The above practices are an abomination to God. An abomination is an intense aversion to or a loathing. It is a vile, shameful or detestable action or condition. *For all who do these things are an abomination to the LORD, and because of these abominations the LORD your God drives them out from before you* (Deuteronomy 18:12).

What Draws People into the Occult?

Oftentimes people are drawn into the occult because of ancestral iniquity. Back in your generational line your ancestors were involved in occultism and created a propensity that was passed on to you. As a kid I grew up in a Christian home where we went to church twice every Sunday, on Wednesday nights, and had family devotions after every evening meal. My family didn't teach me these things but I was drawn into occult activities like water witching, palm reading, tarot cards, hypnosis, magic eight balls and Satanism. Why? Because I inherited a propensity for these kinds of things.

As a mature adult my mother told me the story my grandmother told her. When my grandmother was a little girl her brother got very sick so her parents called in a medium to use her magic arts to bring healing. In her heart grandma knew this was wrong so she spoke out what she was sensing. She said, "This is of the devil." And the medium said, "Well, if the devil can heal what's wrong with that?" This act of my great grandparents brought iniquity into my DNA.

What is a propensity? This illustration may prove helpful. Let's say you find a nest of duck eggs so you take one of those eggs and go to the hen house and put it in the nest of eggs under one of your chickens. The hen hatches out those eggs and the little duckling, along with the other chicks, follow the momma chicken around, scratching and looking for bugs and items to eat. The little duck thinks it's a chicken and so do the other chicks. But one day someone leaves the chicken coop door ajar. The duck makes a beeline for the door and heads to the nearest source of water. Did anyone teach it to swim or to like water? No, it has a propensity for water that was passed to it through its genes. In the same way I inherited a propensity for occultism.

Keep in mind that the SPIRIT OF WITCHCRAFT is different from a witchcraft spirit. The spirit of witchcraft is a more powerful spirit. He is a ruler or a power. He is NOT a principality or a dominion. People who have long generational connection to Divination and Witchcraft must have the iniquity broken in their life.

Occultism in the Church

1 Samuel 15:22,23 states, *For rebellion is as the sin of witchcraft, and stubbornness is as iniquity (wickedness) and idolatry.*

Rebellion permeates the American culture. Outback Steakhouse has as its motto, "No Rules, Just Right." Why did they pick that as their motto? Because it strikes a chord in the heart of the average American. We place high value on our rebellion and independence. We are proud that, "I did it my way." And we bring the rebellion of our culture into the church.

Occultism is usually found in churches and it is manifested through:

rebellion, independence, stubbornness, and manipulation. Sometimes pastors or evangelists will manipulate the people when they appeal for money. They'll say, "God told me that five people are supposed to give $1000," when they really didn't hear from God. Intimidation, domination and control sometimes happen in the church and are symptoms of the spirit of witchcraft.

Witchcraft seeks to control someone else's behavior to do what you want. Witches will use sacrifices, oaths, covenants, curses, spells, potions, drugs and music. But in the church when we try to control other people's lives it is tantamount to witchcraft. Some people seek to control others through false prophetic words, prophecies that didn't originate with God. However, the Bible speaks of the genuine gift of prophecy so don't throw the baby out with the bath water- not all prophecy is evil. The devil will take that which is legitimate and attempt to counterfeit it. Scripture encourages us to test the spirit to see whether it is of God.

Python Spirit

Now it happened, as we went to prayer, that a certain slave girl possessed with a spirit of **divination** *met us, who brought her masters much profit by fortune-telling* (Acts 16:16). The word translated "divination" in this verse is literally the word "python" in the Greek. Remember that divination is the ability to obtain secret knowledge, especially regarding the future. It is the devil's counterfeit of prophecy. The spirit of Python gives divination and witchcraft their inspiration. In the natural, a python kills its prey through constriction and suffocation. Each time its prey takes a breath the python gets a tighter grip. In the spiritual, Python seeks to keep God's people from doing what God's says. Have you ever stepped out to move in the Holy Spirit by faith and something comes to constrict you and hold you back? Have you ever had spiritual apathy and your energy and passion for your ministry has diminished? It could be that Python is trying to deceive you to lose heart and to give up the destiny God has for you. To get rid of Python you must repent, renounce and break all agreements with the various forms of occultism.

Mind Altering Drugs

The word translated as "sorcery" is literally the word *pharmakia* in the New Testament Greek. It's the word from which we get our English word pharmacy or drugs. Notice how it is used in Galatians 5:19-21 which reads, *Now the works of the flesh are evident, which are: adultery, fornication, uncleanness, licentiousness, idolatry, sorcery, hatred, contentions, jealousies, outbursts of wrath, selfish ambitions, dissensions, heresies, envy, murders, drunkenness, revelries, and the like of which I tell you beforehand, just as I also told you in time past, that those who practice such things will not inherit the kingdom of God.*

Illegal drug usage presents a major problem for the Christian who desires to walk in freedom. On the other hand, many decent, church-going individuals get hooked on prescription drugs such as pain killers. The addiction starts out innocently as the person seeks relief from the pain of an injury or other chronic pain. As the treatment continues, very subtly, addiction creeps in and takes over the entire being of the person.

Symptoms of the Occult

- Ears – dumb and deaf spirit
- Eyes – doubt and unbelief

- Throat symptoms are sometimes related to generational Freemasonry
- Mental illness
- Foggy brain syndrome
- Spaced out
- Poor memory
- Band around the head
- Can't talk – go blank – dumb and deaf spirit
- Electromagnetic field sensitivity
- Falling asleep during this Encounter Workshop or when reading the Bible
- Hypersensitivity to sound or smells
- Ringing in the ears
- Easily confused
- Nightmares
- Self-destructiveness
- Insomnia
- Fearfulness

I love the movie, "What About Bob." It's one of my all time favorite movies. The opening scene depicts a multi-phobic individual, Bob Wiley, who has a hard time even getting out of his house. The scene shows him leaving his home to see his new psychologist and as he leaves, he's very careful not to touch any of the walls in the hallway of the apartment complex. He even carries a handkerchief so as not to touch the door knob with his bare hands. He walks out the front door and nervously walks down the front steps. A big bus speeds noisily by separating the viewer from Bob for a few seconds. After the bus clears you see Bob crawling on all fours, frightened by the bus. It is actually a funny scene and we show this brief clip at the Encounter seminar at this point in the teaching on occultism.

We show the movie clip to help lighten things up because the topic of occultism can get heavy. We also show it to call attention to the problem of fear. Fear remains a huge problem for humankind but many fears begin with occultism. Occultism and fear go hand in hand.

Fear and the Occult

*Now Samuel had died, and all Israel had lamented for him and buried him in Ramah, in his own city. And Saul had put the mediums and the spiritists out of the land. Then the Philistines gathered together, and came and encamped at Shunem. So Saul gathered all Israel together, and they encamped at Gilboa. When Saul saw the army of the Philistines, he was **afraid**, and his heart trembled greatly. And when Saul inquired of the LORD, the LORD did not answer him, either by dreams or by Urim or by the prophets. Then Saul said to his servants, "Find me a woman who is a medium, that I may go to her and inquire of her." And his servants said to him, "In fact, there is a woman who is a **medium** at En Dor."* (1 Samuel 28:3-7).

Notice the connection between Saul's fear and his seeking a medium. It is impossible to rid your life of fear if you have not dealt with occultism. Fear and the spirit of occultism weave themselves together to hold each other in place. Occultism fuels fear and fear fuels occultism. Fear pushes a person into occultism and fear is also a byproduct of occultism.

Jeanie's husband, Ron, was diagnosed with an aggressive inoperable brain tumor and was given a maximum of two months to live. She asked her church to put Ron's name on the prayer chain. After word got out about their crisis, an acquaintance told Jeanie about a psychic healer in Mexico who was famous for miraculous cures. The healer often used an unsterilized knife and performed operations while in a trance-like state. The incisions she made healed almost immediately and she had a high success rate with terminal cases. Jeanie's heart told her something was wrong but out of desperation and fear she packed the car and drove her husband to the little town just across the border. "After all," she reasoned, "The prayer chain hasn't worked so far and God must somehow be involved in guiding the psychic healer because only God can heal." Fear drove her to do something her heart said was wrong.

Sadly, the church in America, by-in-large, is devoid of supernatural power. Consequently, people are drawn to the occult because there they find the supernatural manifestations to help them cope with life. Psychic healing, even though it may produce results, stands in contradiction to the Word of God. Should Christians involve themselves in various forms of occultism simply because they work? Occult practices may work but they bring with them new fears that the person never bargained for.

Jeanie's husband was miraculously healed by the psychic healer. His quick recovery astonished everyone, especially his doctor. But as the months went by Jeanie developed debilitating panic attacks. Her doctor prescribed medications to keep the symptoms somewhat bearable but soon other fears began to surface. She feared that a terminal illness might strike her or one of her children. She feared her own death and experienced recurring night terrors. Soon she faced her worst nightmare. Ron's tumor came back more aggressively than before and he died a month after the new diagnosis.

God has our best interest in mind when He commands us to avoid involvement in the occult. The Bible strictly forbids all practices

Trap Number Five: Occultic Influence

that relate to occultism. When the children of Israel prepared to take possession of the Promised Land God gave this warning, *When you come into the land which the LORD your God is giving you, you shall not learn to follow the abominations of those nations. There shall not be found among you anyone who makes his son or his daughter pass through the fire, or one who practices witchcraft, or a soothsayer, or one who interprets omens, or a sorcerer, or one who conjures spells, or a medium, or a spiritist, or one who calls up the dead. For all who do these things are an abomination to the LORD, and because of these abominations the LORD your God drives them out from before you. You shall be blameless before the LORD your God. For these nations which you will dispossess listened to soothsayers and diviners; but as for you, the LORD your God has not appointed such for you* (Deuteronomy 18:9-14).

Unfortunately many Christians open the door to evil influences unintentionally because of lack of knowledge in this area. Satan doesn't care if you innocently play with something related to divination. But when you do, you give him permission to gain a certain amount of leverage in your life. For example, many children play with the magic eight ball not realizing that this is a form of divination. Others out of curiosity read their horoscope without taking it seriously. It doesn't matter whether or not you believe in astrology. What counts is that you gave the devil legal ground and you need to remove it through repentance and renunciation.

Here is a list of evidences that occultism exists in your life. Sometimes people inherit a propensity toward occultism through the sins of their ancestors. Circle any that you have done at any time in your life whether you did them as an adult or a child. Also circle any you know of that your parents, grandparents, or great grandparents were involved in because the effects of these things get passed on for at least four generations.

- independence
- mediums
- horoscopes
- rebellion
- stubbornness
- Satanism (worship of Satan)
- the reading of tea leaves
- domination
- diviners
- astrology / Ouija boards
- séances
- white witchcraft
- channeling
- Tarot cards
- worship of ancestral spirits
- psychic healers
- ungodly covenants
- New Age involvement
- white magic
- Voodoo
- palm readers
- games
    (Masters of the Universe, Dungeons & Dragons, Magic Eight Ball, Pokemon, crystal balls, etc.)
- Santeria
- mysticism
- transcendental meditation
- mood altering drugs

Trap Number Five: Occultic Influence

unscriptural attempts at deliverance
    (Those that do not line up with the Word)

fortune-tellers

Freemasonry or secret organizations

Eastern religions

water witching

pendulums

control

levitation

manipulation

black magic

mental telepathy

To this list I would like to add yoga because I am disturbed to see so many Christians involved in this counterfeit attempt to gain peace. Those who promote yoga say that it facilitates peace and inner tranquility. I believe that it does just the opposite. Several knowledgeable people have told me that their experience is that those who continue to practice this ancient form of Hinduism actually find it increasingly more difficult to resist stress. This is because any unscriptural attempt to achieve peace gives the enemy an inroad.

Read carefully the following quotations to help you understand the heart of the problem. Yoga is clearly a form or an expression of religion. "As we have said, many who recommend yoga claim it is an excellent way in which to loosen one's muscles, keep fit, and maintain health. For these people, yoga is simply physical exercise and nothing more; the practice has little to do with religion. Such persons, however, do not properly understand the nature and purpose of true yoga practice. Yoga is much more than merely an innocent form of relaxing the mind and body. One reason that yoga clearly belongs in the category of religion is because the classic yoga texts reveal that proper yoga practice incorporates many goals of occultism. Allegedly, it will not only result in a "sound" mind and a "healthy" body, but also in spiritual (occult) enlightenment." [3]

The physical exercises of yoga are believed to prevent diseases and maintain health through the regulation of *prana* or mystical life energy. David Fetcho, an authority in yoga theory and practice, states: "Physical yoga, according to its classical definitions, is inheritably and functionally incapable of being separated from Eastern religious metaphysics. The Western practitioner who attempts to do so is operating in ignorance and danger, from the yogi's viewpoint, as well as from the Christian." [4]

The doctrine of kundalini should also raise some concerns. "In Hindu mythology, the serpent goddess *kundalini* 'rests' at the base of the spine. She is aroused by yoga practice, travels up the spine while regulating prana and opening the body's alleged psychic centers (*chakras*), finally reaching the top (crown) *chakra*, permitting the merging of Shiva/Shakti and occult enlightenment."[5]   I don't know about you but I don't want a serpent goddess traveling up my back!

Activating the Kundalini is not, as commonly thought, restricted to *hatha* yoga. Yoga authorities themselves have said that all yoga is fundamentally kundalini yoga and that yoga is senseless without it. This is why no less an authority than Hans Reiker concludes, "Kundalini is the mainstay of *all* yoga practices."[6]

Yoga is used as a basic means of achieving an altered state of consciousness. "Altered states of consciousness (ASCs) in a New Age context comprise unusual conditions of perception achieved by the deliberate cultivation of often abnormal mental states, states not normally experienced apart from specific religious techniques and/or occult programs."[7]   The amygdala, the part of the brain that places you in space gets shut down during an altered state of consciousness. When this happens you will experience a feeling of being without boundaries.

Trap Number Five: Occultic Influence

Most people believe that Yoga is merely a program for teaching proper breathing and stretching techniques. In actuality, it is designed to produce a mystical experience. Ernest L. Rossi of the Department of Psychology at UCLA asserts that yoga is designed to induce altered states of consciousness. "If one considers the ancient yoga science of *pranayama* (controlled breathing) to have relevance, then one must admit that the manual manipulation of the nasal cycle during meditation (*dhyana*) is the most thoroughly documented of techniques for altering consciousness. For thousands of years these techniques for the subtle alterations of nasal breathing have been gradually codified into classical texts..."[8]

The goal of the yogi is the realization that all is one—in other words, no boundaries. This tenant represents a world view, known as monism, is contrary to Scripture and undermines the teaching of the gospel. Jesus came to save us from our sins so that we might be brought into relationship with God. He didn't come to merely enlighten us. The consequences for involvement in yoga are that the door gets opened to evil spirits, one is easily influenced by surroundings, and one takes on the physical symptoms and mind states of other people. *He that has no rule over his own spirit is like a city that is broken down, and without walls* (Proverbs 25:28).

In addition, one of the most insidious forms of divination is Freemasonry. Those who join its ranks usually do not understand the full extent of the evil revealed in the higher degrees. Once a Freemason reaches the 33rd degree he learns that the Great Architect of the Universe is none other than Lucifer himself. People often protest when I teach on this subject. "My grandfather was a Mason and he was a good person." My response to that objection is, "He may have been a good person but he was deceived in this area." I do not deny that Masons do a lot of good.

As a little boy Clyde badly burned his leg. The doctors did their best but after months of treatment they said they would have to amputate. Then someone on his behalf contacted the Shriners, a Masonic organization that does much to help individuals with medical problems. They admitted Clyde into their hospital and paid the hefty bill accrued through months of intensive treatments. Eventually his leg healed and Clyde was forever grateful. For the rest of his life Clyde never missed a chance to tell people about the kindness the Shriners demonstrated to him.

With testimonies like Clyde's it often proves difficult to convince people that Freemasonry is another form of occultism. Keep in mind that Masonry is not a Christian organization because its teachings do not line up with the Word of God. "Masonry is not based on the Bible (referred to as "The Great Light"), but on the Kabala, the ultimate source of Masonic beliefs (Morals and Dogma), which is a medieval book of mysticism and magic. Masons require one to believe in God to be a member, but the candidate is never required to say what god he believes in. Masons commonly refer to their deity as the "Great Architect of the Universe" (G.A.O.T.U.) or the Supreme Being. The name of Christ is seldom referred to in Masonic literature, apparently due to Masons not wanting to offend their non-Christian members. Freemasonry does not believe that Jesus Christ is God, nor that salvation is available only through Him.

Bill Keller stated that, "The reality of sin in the Biblical sense is denied. Masons think that any 'shortcomings' can be overcome by greater enlightenment. Because they deny the reality of sin, Masons see no need for salvation in the Biblical sense. They see salvation as a step-by-step enlightenment, which comes through initiation into the Masonic degrees and their mysteries."[9]

If Freemasonry runs in your background I encourage you to thoroughly renounce it. Some specific Masonic organizations include the women's Orders of the Eastern Star, the White Shrine of Jerusalem, the girl's order of the Daughters of the Eastern Star, the International Orders of Job's Daughters, Rainbow Girls, and the boy's Order of DeMolay.

At a seminar a lady became angry and vehemently challenged the teaching that opposed Freemasonry. Then during the lunch break she decided to pray the prayer of renunciation found in the back of the syllabus just to see what would happen. As she prayed she suddenly got violently sick and threw up her lunch. Every time she attempted to resume the prayer she got ill all over again. Needless to say, it became apparent to her that something was dreadfully wrong. After the lunch break she anxiously awaited ministry and was in total agreement that Freemasonry had to go. (A prayer of release from Freemasonry is found in the appendix at the back of the book.)

In 2 Corinthians 11:3-4 we read, *But I fear, lest by any means, as the serpent beguiled Eve through his subtlety, so your minds should be corrupted from the simplicity that is in Christ. For if he that comes preaches another Jesus, whom we have not preached, or if you receive another spirit, which you have not received, or another gospel, which you have not accepted, you might well bear with him.* This Scripture passage clearly teaches that there is another Jesus, another Spirit, and another Gospel, so don't be fooled just because they throw around some familiar terms.

At times good and evil look very much alike and the only way you know the difference is by the Spirit of God and the Scriptures. Every cult somehow lays claim to Jesus so just because they use the name of Jesus doesn't indicate that they mean the same thing we do when we refer to Christ.

Prayer

Other occultic practices exist that need to be renounced and repented of. They include but are not limited to the following list. Please repeat after me out loud as a group. "I confess and repent for both my own and my ancestors' use of pendulums in foretelling the future, reading of tea leaves, trusting in fetishes or charms, psychic readings, table tipping, clairvoyance, astrology, ESP, 'third eye', mental telepathy, the use of spirit guides, necromancy (communication with the dead), out of body experiences, astral projection, Druidism (if your ancestors came from Britain,

Germany, France and or in the vicinity), automatic handwriting, palm reading, metaphysics, mysticism, spiritism, worship of ancestral spirits, belief in reincarnation, visiting non-Christian supernatural faith healers, the worship of idols, consulting with witch doctors, shamanism, Santeria, psychic healers, New Age doctrine, Eastern religions, yoga, mantras, Transcendental Meditation, hypnosis, Freemasonry, levitation, white magic, black magic, voodoo, demonic games such as Charlie Charlie, Dungeons and Dragons, Masters of the Universe, World of WarCraft, Magic: The Gathering, Ouija boards, and Bloody Mary, mood altering drug dependence, sorcery, water witching, casting spells, incantations, curses, hexes, vexes, ungodly vows and oaths, ungodly covenants, blood sacrifices, animal sacrifices, human sacrifices, control, intimidation, manipulation, domination and playing with crystal balls and eight balls. I decree and declare that the blood covenant I have with Jesus Christ of Nazareth, supersedes all other covenants made by me and my ancestors. Based on Isaiah 28:18, I ask You Father, to annul any ungodly covenants that would hold me in bondage to the occult and break any agreements with Sheol. I reject, renounce, and break all agreements with these practices, in Jesus' Name, Amen."

CHAPTER SEVEN
Trap Number Six: Curses

Curses represent another powerful trap the enemy sets for us on our pathway to freedom. Curses impede us from walking out our God ordained destiny. The word "curse" is used 165 times in the New King James Version of the Bible. This number increases slightly depending on the translation you look in. My point is this: if God uses the term between 165 and 175 times in His Word then it must be an important topic to Him and we should take it seriously.

In the Old Testament God said that if the Children of Israel refused to obey Him they would be under a curse. *Behold, I set before you today a blessing and a curse: the blessing, if you obey the commandments of the LORD your God which I command you today; and the curse, if you do not obey the commandments of the LORD your God, but turn aside from the way which I command you today, to go after other gods which you have not known* (Deuteronomy 11:26-28). In Deuteronomy 28:15 we read, *But it shall come to pass, if you do not obey the voice of the LORD your God, to observe carefully all His commandments and His statutes which I command you today, that all these curses will come upon you and overtake you.* This same chapter goes on to present a very extensive list of curses that come through disobedience. The lesson is simply this: obedience to God protects us from curses and disobedience invites curses.

When I bring up the subject of curses I often encounter Christians' objections and they say, "Christ has redeemed me from the curse of the law having been made a curse for me." They are referencing Galatians 3:13 and that is true. They go on to say, "When I got saved Jesus took care of all that business so that's all in my past. I don't have to deal with it because Jesus already did." However, they fail to pay attention to the rest of that Scripture passage which reads, *that the blessing of Abraham might come upon the Gentiles in Christ Jesus, that we might receive the promise of the Spirit through faith* (Galatians 3:14). All of the blessings that have been provided for us through the finished work of Christ have to be put into effect through faith.

Jesus may have died for all but all people are not automatically saved. Only those who put their faith in him will be saved. In the same way we must apply the finished work of Calvary by faith to break curses. I count four times in the Bible where it says, "The just shall live by faith." For example, in Romans 1:17 we read, *For in it the righteousness of God is revealed from* **faith** *to* **faith***; as it is written,* **"The just shall live by faith**.*"* (emphasis added). We have to apply faith to all the promises of God, we don't just automatically receive the benefits of Christ's redemptive work.

The Curse of Illegitimacy

One of the most prevalent types of curses is the curse of illegitimacy. "Illegitimate" refers to one conceived out of wedlock, not that they lack legitimacy as a human being, nor that God didn't purpose their existence but it is a curse that carries consequences brought on by our sins and the sins of those in our bloodline. This curse began back in the Old Testament where we read, *One of illegitimate birth shall not enter the assembly of the LORD; even to the tenth generation none of his descendants shall enter the assembly of the LORD* (Deuteronomy 23:2).

One of illegitimate birth could not worship with their countrymen in the court of the Israelites. They had to stay on the outside in the court of the Gentiles. This law meant that if they were of the priestly tribe they were not allowed to serve in the inner courts and the curse went on, generation after generation, for 10 generations. If a generation was 40 years then it continued on for 400 hundred years so what is the likelihood that this curse operates in your life? The probability is high. That's why I encourage everyone to break it even if their parents were married when they were conceived because it runs generationally. If the curse is not present in your life it won't hurt you to have someone pray to break this curse, but if it does exist, the prayer will help you a lot. Let's just assume that it is present.

We, as New Testament believers, are not under the Old Testament ceremonial law but the curse still operates today. This curse causes a person to feel like they don't belong, like they are on the outside looking in. The curse can also obstruct a would-be worshipper from moving into the presence of God. They feel like it's hard to connect with God on an intimate level. If none of these symptoms seem to exist in your life I still recommend that you break the curse because doing so will make it even easier to connect with God and others.

Associated with this curse we find condemnation, false guilt, false responsibility, and shame. The human spirit comes downloaded with tons of information at the moment of conception. At conception the human spirit understands the language of the biological parents and caregivers and can deeply feel the pain and rejection of negative words. If the parents are ashamed of their sin of premarital sex and try to hide the fact that they got pregnant out of wedlock, the unborn child takes on that shame. It's easy for the devil to implant the lie in their heart that they are shameful. Sometimes a pregnancy causes a couple to believe they have to get married right away. The rushed marriage often disrupts career or educational plans and, as the parents talk about their disappointments, the child hears it all and takes on a sense of false responsibility. They believe the lie that it's their fault that their parent's life goals were disrupted. If the unwed parents worry that they don't have the financial resources to support a child, the unborn child may feel the condemnation of putting financial pressure on the parents. The list goes on but here are a few examples of how destructive lies get planted.

Prayer to Break the Curse of Illegitimacy

"Heavenly Father, I agree with You that the curse of illegitimacy functions in my generational bloodline and in me. I confess my sin (only confess your own sin if it applies) and the sin of my ancestors for having sex outside of marriage. I ask that You break this curse and help me connect more fully with You and with others. I reject, renounce and break all agreements with condemnation, false guilt, false responsibility, rejection, and shame. I ask that You, Father, would remove all these lies of the enemy, in Jesus' Name, Amen."

Next, the prayer minister prays, "In the name of Jesus I take authority over the curse of illegitimacy and command it to get off your life. I take authority over condemnation, false guilt, false responsibility, rejection, and shame that came with illegitimacy and command them to leave now. I declare that this curse is broken off you now in Jesus' Name. Now I gather up your spirit outside the camp and I pull your spirit into the camp. You are no longer in the outer courts. I pull your spirit into the inner courts and into the very presence of God, right where you belong. I bond your spirit to the Spirit Jehovah God, the Creator of the ends of the earth and I say, 'Welcome home, child of God,' in Jesus' Name, Amen."

Word Curses

Word curses represent another very common type of curse. Proverbs 18:21 reads, *Death and life are in the power of the tongue, and those who love it will eat its fruit*. When God says this He really means it. The spoken word has the power to bring death or life. The old adage, "Sticks and stones may break my bones but words will never hurt me" is just untrue. The negative, caustic, accusatory words of others can set our lives on a destructive path. The enemy knows the power of the tongue so he seeks to set this trap for our lives. Negative words spoken by those in authority over us, such as parents, grandparents, teachers, or pastors carry especially powerful weight. Words such as, "You'll never amount to anything." "You're as dumb as dirt." "You're as worthless as ...." "You're lazy." "You're a slut." "You're just like...." and "You're a bum just like your dad." "Why can't you be smart like your sister?" release demonic energy to keep us in bondage.

And don't forget to consider the negative words you've spoken over yourself. You set the course of your life by what comes out of your mouth. *Indeed, we put bits in horses' mouths that they may obey us, and we turn their whole body. Look also at ships: although they are so large and are driven by fierce winds, they are turned by a very small rudder wherever the pilot desires. Even so the tongue is a little member and boasts great things* (James 3:3-5).

Prayer to Break Word Curses

"Heavenly Father, I take authority over all negative words spoken against me and I cast them down to the ground. I reject, renounce, and break all agreements I've ever made with those words. Any demons assigned to me through those words I re-assign to dry places now, in Jesus' Name. I ask You Lord to pull up all the pain those words may have caused, flush out the poison of these words, and bring Your healing, in Jesus' Name, Amen."

The Death Curse

The enemy uses the Death Curse to bring death to your physical body, death to your finances, death to your relationships, death to your career, death to your ministry, death to your dreams, and death to your God-given destiny. After all, the devil comes to steal, kill, and destroy. *The thief does not come except to steal, and to kill, and to destroy. I have come that they may have life, and that they may have it more abundantly* (John 10:10).

How do you know whether or not you have this curse in operation? Here are a few indicators: a) near fatal accidents, b) life-threatening illnesses, c) your mother had a miscarriage prior to having you, d) your mother attempted to abort you, e) words of death were spoken over you by someone in authority, for example, dad says to your mom, "I hope the baby miscarries." You obviously would not remember this incident but the story may have been told to you. f) the cord was wrapped around your neck at birth, g) involvement in Freemasonry, h) you had an abortion or aided another person in getting an abortion, i) words of death spoken over yourself such as, "I wish I was dead." j) strong suicidal thoughts, and k) suicidal attempts.

Trap Number Six: Curses

Prayer to Break the Death Curse

"Almighty God, the Lord and Giver of Life, I confess the sin of my ancestors for submitting to Satan's system and allowing the Death Curse entry into my generational bloodline. I confess my sin of _____ (name the following sins you have committed) strong suicidal thoughts, attempted suicide, aborting a baby, aiding another in getting an abortion, speaking words of death over myself, and involvement in Freemasonry (or any other organization where you speak death curses over yourself if you divulge its secrets). I receive Your forgiveness and the blood of Jesus cleanses me now. I break all agreements with the death curse and I command the death curse to leave me now, in Jesus' Name. Heavenly Father, I ask that You would cut off any of the death curse that may be coming against me from the second heaven. Now I declare the life of Christ over me. Jesus came to give me life and life more abundantly and I receive His life, in Jesus' Name, Amen."

The Curse of Molech

Molech was a god that was worshipped by various people groups in Biblical days. The idol was formed out of cast iron with a hollowed out belly opened in the front. Its arms were extended outward, perpendicular to its body, and its hands turned upward. They would build a red hot fire in its belly and place their newborn baby into its outstretched arms. Then they would commence to indulge in sexual orgies while the baby cooked to death. Needless to say, God considered this rite to be an abomination in His sight and this heinous sin opened the door for the Curse of Molech to all who participated.

I am not aware of any practicing of overt worship to the idol Molech going on today but, nevertheless, millions of people have brought the curse on themselves through abortion. The curse brings with it financial lack, aimlessness, lack of direction, and devastation. I don't write these words to bring condemnation to those who have had abortions but to offer freedom. If you confess this sin, God totally forgives and forgets but its effects can continue on unless you break this curse.

Prayer to Break the Curse of Molech

Keep in mind that as you pray, the god Molech is probably a second-heaven entity. We don't have direct authority to bring down second-heaven entities, that is not our domain. Instead, we need to ask God to deal with the Curse of Molech at the second-heaven level. "Heavenly Father, I confess my sin of having an abortion and/or aiding another person in getting an abortion. I agree with You that it was sin and I now receive Your forgiveness. I forgive myself just because You have already forgiven me. I ask You now Father to loose the Curse of Molech from me at the second-heaven level. I break this curse off me at this level, in Jesus' Name. Please remove from me all of the effects of this curse including financial lack, aimlessness, lack of direction, and devastation, in Jesus' Name, Amen.

Witchcraft Curses

Whether we like it or not, the truth is that witchcraft is real and many witches and warlocks possess great power. You say, "Well, I don't concern myself with that. I'm a born again Christian." I say to you, "You may be genuinely born again but if there is any cause in you whatsoever, the curse may alight." In Proverbs 26:2 we read, *Like a flitting sparrow, like a flying swallow, so a curse without cause shall not alight*. This verse implies that if there is a cause the curse may alight. The cause may not be your own sin but a generational sin or iniquity that you've never dealt with.

Witches and warlocks are very dedicated to send curses against churches and Christian leaders. They like to focus on the breakup of the leader's marriage and family and to impede the success and effectiveness of the local church. Sadly, many witches are more committed to what they do than Christians are to advance the Kingdom of God.

Years ago, when I was pastoring a church in Southern California, I got up in the morning, went to the church, and everything I did was a struggle. It felt as though I was walking in water up to my neck. Have you ever tried to walk very fast in high water? It takes a lot of effort. The resistance continued until mid afternoon until I was so exhausted I cried out to God, "Lord, what's wrong? What have I done? Have I sinned?" And the Lord answered me quite clearly. He said, "They're praying against you My son." That was a revelation. I had never considered that as a possibility but, out of faith, I began to pray to break and cancel those prayers. As I did, almost immediately, I experienced an atmospheric change. The room seemed to lighten and the heavy weight was broken off. I felt free to function as normal.

I learned a valuable lesson that day, and that is that there are people diligently praying against pastors and other church leaders. Over the years, about every two years or so, I had repeat experiences like the one just described. I finally came to the realization that I need to deal with this issue on a daily basis as a part of my routine spiritual hygiene.

I think of a dear friend of mine who makes frequent trips to the remote people groups in Africa and other parts of the world. He is a powerful man of God, operating in signs and wonders. He has much of the Bible committed to memory and regularly leads people in prayer to receive Christ. On one of his mission trips years ago he got tangled up with a witch doctor. When he got back to the states his head was spinning. In spite of the fact that he is a spiritual giant he still needed to visit a powerful prayer ministry to get that junk broken off him. If he needed it, then most of us need to deal with the issue of witchcraft curses as well.

Prayer to Break Witchcraft Curses

"I take authority over all hexes, vexes, spells, curses, gossip, psychic/soulish prayers, negative confession, voodoo, hoodoo, Satanism, Santeria, Muslim prayers, Freemasonry curses and prayers, and witchcraft used against me. I bind and break the power of these things and cast them down to the ground. Any demons assigned to me through these endeavors I reassign to dry places now, in Jesus' Name. I cut off any witch or warlock who is cursing me from accessing future powers of darkness and I ask you God to save and bless the witch or warlock, in Jesus' Name, Amen." Begin praising God for His victory and wait until you get a peace or release in your spirit that it is done.

The Lynching Curse

African-Americans whose ancestors served as slaves usually inherit the lynching curse. During the days of slavery in America, Willie Lynch was hired by plantation owners to rein in rebellious slaves by intimidating them through open hangings. We have found that the bondage of what those slaves experienced got passed on genetically to their descendants. Here is the testimony of an African-American who received ministry in this area.

> *As an African American, there was a time in my life where I would not have been open to the possibility of a lynching curse that likely impacts a significant percentage of the*

African American population descending from slavery. As a matter of fact with an upbringing rooted in Christianity and cultural pride where faith, focus, hard work, and community equaled success, there was no place for the excuses of past ethnic pains to thwart present and future progress. No time to mourn. We were the generation following Dr. King. There was a baton to carry, a torch to keep lit.

As for me, I excelled in private parochial school from pre-k through college, and on to dual masters' work, etc. I added these only to state that in spite of my qualifications there were goals, destiny, purpose that I simply could not reach. Now I had no problem excelling in and did enjoy a flourishing career. But whenever it came to stepping up into what I knew to be destiny I was hit with tremendous fright and a subconscious sense that there seemed to be something forbidding it. I remember thinking if I could just see this invisible foe then I could stand it down. I knew it was a part of me in some way or the other.

As far back as I can remember, as an adult, there would be times when I experienced a presence about my neck. I recall using my hand as to quickly brush it away. At other times I would make a rapid movement that involved shrugging my shoulders and turning my head in a subconscious effort to shake loose from the sense of an invisible collar on my neck. One prominent instance comes to mind.

In November 2004, I was on the phone ministering in prayer to someone. As the Holy Spirit began to move in revelation and in breaking bondages, I began to lightly sense that presence about my neck. I kept right on praying determined that the Holy Spirit would not be interrupted. The more fervent and effectual the prayer became the more intense the presence became. By the time the prayer and conversation had ended I remember the hold being so tight that I literally began gasping for breath and sinking down in the bed where I was sitting. I was unable to cry out for help. Whispering, I repeatedly uttered, 'the Blood of Jesus,' until I was freed from it. What was only a few moments, seemed to me an hour. I was visibly shaken.

In June of 2007, I attended a Vision Life Ministries', Freedom and Fullness seminar. I was asked if anyone had ever ministered to me in the area of breaking the lynching curse. The seminar leader proceeded to explain who Willie Lynch was, and that the purpose of the curse was to prevent African Americans with slavery lineage from rising up into their God given destiny and purpose. It was my eureka moment. I knew that the presence that would come and go about my neck, that invisible collar, was the lynching curse. I received prayer ministry and that curse was broken from my life and destiny that day. Today I walk in the ministry that God has blueprinted for me. This is my destiny. -KD

If you are not of African-American descent don't think that you are automatically immune to this curse. I have found that individuals of various ethnicity suffer from this curse especially if their ancestors suffered subjugation like that of the African-Americans. The term "Lynching Curse" is only a name, a designation that the kingdom of darkness responds to, even if technically your ancestors weren't threatened with hanging. They may have been brought into submission by other means. I also discovered that white people whose ancestors were slave owners often carry this curse.

Prayer to Break the Lynching Curse

Leader prays, "In the name of Jesus, I break the lynching curse off of you. I pull off this noose around your neck and give it to Jesus for His disposal. (Symbolically remove the noose from around their neck with a hand motion.) I pull off all the chains and bondages that came through this curse and give them to Jesus for

His disposal. (Use a symbolic hand motion to pull off the chains and bondages from around their feet and ankles and off their arms and torso.) I command any demons assigned to you through this curse to go to dry places right now and never return. I pull up the iniquity of the lynching curse out of your body and your DNA."

The Janteloven Curse

The Janteloven Curse affects people with a Scandinavian heritage. The following prayer of renunciation includes some of the "laws" that most Scandinavians are aware govern their society. Not only Scandinavia (Norway, Sweden, etc.) but the places that the people of Scandinavia have settled have been affected culturally by it. In the United States, some of our states such as Minnesota, Wisconsin, North and South Dakota, and others have also been affected by these beliefs. These represent one of the major strongholds that hinder many Scandinavians from coming into their fullness as believers. And like in the epistle of Titus, these "laws" were noted in 1933 by a Danish writer, Akaei Sandemose, a Scandinavian – one of their own.

While the Janteloven is in effect, there will be a lid on worship because if you are more expressive than someone else you might be breaking part of the law. There can be no "honor to whom honor is due," because you should not think that you are more important than another. The apostles and other five-fold gifts cannot rise up because they might fancy themselves to be better than others.

Prayer to Renounce the Janteloven Curse (Scandinavian Curses)

"I break, shatter, cut-off, dissolve and destroy the curse that says I am not special.

I break, shatter, cut-off, dissolve and destroy the curse that says I do not have the same standing as others.

I break, shatter, cut-off, dissolve and destroy the curse that says others are smarter than me.

I break, shatter, cut-off, dissolve and destroy the curse that says others are better than me.

I break, shatter, cut-off, dissolve and destroy the curse that says others know more than I do.

I break, shatter, cut-off, dissolve and destroy the curse that says others are more important than I am.

I break, shatter, cut-off, dissolve and destroy the curse that says I am not good at anything.

I break, shatter, cut-off, dissolve and destroy the curse that says that I will not laugh in public.

I break, shatter, cut-off, dissolve and destroy the curse that says no one cares about me.

I break, shatter, cut-off, dissolve and destroy the curse that says I cannot be taught anything."[10]

Vietnam Curse

Many of our soldiers were shipped to Vietnam to fight that war only to return to the United States with their lives in upheaval. They face the scourge that so often affects our GI's known as Post Traumatic Stress Disorder. In addition to PTSD they face another force that the secular medical world knows little of. It is called the Vietnam Curse. An ex-Buddhist priest has revealed that an entire sect of Vietnamese Buddhist monks dedicated themselves to pray and invoke curses upon our GI's. They spent years diligently sending curses that our men would become wandering individuals for the rest of their lives, that they would never find peace, and that they would be angry people for the rest of their lives.

Prayer to Break the Vietnam Curse

"In the name of Jesus Christ of Nazareth, I take authority over the Vietnam Curse made against me. I reject, renounce and cancel any agreements I ever made with this curse. I cast all these curses on me down to the ground. I declare that the Vietnam Curse is broken off me now in Jesus' Name. I break the curse that says that I would wander the rest of my life, that I would never find peace, and that I would be angry for the rest of my life, in Jesus' Mighty Name, Amen."

Gulf War Curse

Similar to the Vietnam Curse many of our soldiers were cursed, not by Buddhist monks but by Muslims. Muslims are quite adept at invoking curses on Americans.

Prayer to Break The Gulf War Curse

"In the name of Jesus Christ of Nazareth, I take authority over the Gulf War Curse made against me. I reject, renounce and cancel any agreements I ever made with the effects of this curse. I cast all these curses on me down to the ground. I declare that the Gulf War Curse is broken off me now in Jesus' Name."

CHAPTER EIGHT
Trap Number Seven: Trauma

The Spirit of the Lord GOD is upon Me, because the LORD has anointed Me to preach good tidings to the poor; He has sent Me to heal the brokenhearted, to proclaim liberty to the captives, and the opening of the prison to those who are bound; to proclaim the acceptable year of the LORD, and the day of vengeance of our God; to comfort all who mourn, to console those who mourn in Zion, to give them beauty for ashes, the oil of joy for mourning, the garment of praise for the spirit of heaviness; that they may be called trees of righteousness, the planting of the LORD, that He may be glorified (Isaiah 61:1-3).

These verses refer to Jesus Christ and it's obvious that a major part of Jesus' ministry was to heal our inner wounds. The Bible says that He is the same yesterday, today, and forever so He's still in the ministry of healing our broken hearts.

Here are some examples of trauma that many people experience:

1. Accidents

    a. Automobile accidents can cause great trauma especially in children.

b. Job-related accidents. My dad was at work one day and a co-worker got his arm caught in some machinery. It pulled his arm off and he bled out almost instantly. Those kind of things can produce trauma for those who witness them.

c. Other accidents. My wife, Ruthie, and I went with our kids to Southern California to visit her mother. While we were there we thought we'd take advantage of being so close to Disneyland. We spent all day at Disneyland and came back to grandma's house quite exhausted. We put the kids to bed, my five-year old son on the top bunk and his younger sister on the bottom.

We went to bed for some much-needed sleep. In the middle of the night we were abruptly awakened by the sound of a bloodcurdling scream. We ran into the kids' bedroom only to see my son, Jeremy, on the floor, the bone sticking out of his bicep, and blood everywhere. He had fallen out of the top bunk and hit his arm on the dresser on the way down. Grandma called the paramedics while I put my hand on his arm and prayed, concerned that he was losing a lot of blood. Within a few minutes the bleeding stopped. The paramedics arrived and rushed him to the hospital. A neurosurgeon was called in to do emergency surgery. After he examined my son he walked into the waiting room where grandma, Ruthie, and I sat anxiously waiting for his assessment. He said, "Mr. and Mrs. Frye, this is the worse break in the upper body that I've ever seen in all my years as a neurosurgeon. I don't know if we'll be able to save his arm."

The surgery commenced as we said a brief prayer. My mother-in-law and Ruthie started to chat about every inane subject imaginable like shopping, hair products and sewing. Finally, out of frustration, I impatiently cut into their conversation and said, "How can you just sit here and talk? We should be praying." In hindsight I think they actually had more real faith than I did at the time.

After what seemed to be an eternity, the surgeon came back in the waiting room. He said, "We were able to pin the bones together and sew up the tear in his bicep but the nerve was stretched so much that I don't know if he'll ever be able to use his arm again. In addition, the bone was so exposed that it's likely that infection will set in and he'll lose his arm anyway." This procedure took place in the era when the powerful antibiotics of today were not available.

We stayed in the hospital for several days as my son recuperated. After the first day we watched my son's thumb move just a little. The next day his index finger moved. And the third day all of his fingers moved ever so slightly but we rejoiced in the knowledge that the nerve was still alive and we thanked God for the miracle. It gradually became apparent that he was free from the danger of infection - another praise the Lord. So we made our way back home to Northern California with Jeremy's arm in a big cast and pins sticking out of his elbow and bicep.

After a period of about six weeks, we made the trip to Crescent City where we had a follow-up doctor's appointment. After taking x-rays they cut the cast off and pulled out the pins - a gruesome sight for a father. They put his arm in a sling with a soft cast around it for support. On the way home we decided to stop at our friends' house for a visit, knowing that our children would like that because our friends had two young children also. Upon arrival, the kids went out into the back yard while the adults stayed inside to visit. After a few minutes we heard a bloodcurdling scream coming from the back yard. We ran out there to discover my son's arm swollen to the size of a watermelon. He had fallen down and rebroke his arm. We rushed him back to the hospital where they put him into another hard cast. By this time my nerves were frazzled. We drove home and the family went inside while I went over to our church to pray. I went into the worship center to pour out my heart to God. I said, "Lord, I don't know if I can handle this thing of being a parent." I know this experience was traumatic for my son but I think I was actually more traumatized than he was and I needed healing from the trauma.

2. Abandonment. When a man leaves his wife for another woman it creates a deep wound in her. When a mother or father abandons their child it leaves a deep wound of rejection and may manifest itself in anger and rebellion. Adopted children typically feel deep abandonment even though their new parents love them deeply. In this case it often proves helpful to sever the soul tie from their biological parents so they can bond more easily with their adoptive parents. Abandonment leads to the fear of abandonment and this fear can open the door to a host of physical maladies such as allergies.

Several years after our marriage Ruthie developed a severe allergy to corn. The least little bit of a corn product sent her running to the bathroom to vomit. They put corn in nearly all packaged foods, soft drinks, cereal and casseroles so she had to watch very carefully what she ate. I would sometimes teasingly ask her if she wanted a bag of popcorn or a piece of corn on the cob, but all teasing aside, I truly felt sorry for her.

Then one day she received ministry in the area of abandonment. When she was around two years old her father was killed fighting a forest fire as a volunteer. This tragedy left her mother alone to raise her four children. The wound of her father's loss created fertile soil for the enemy to plant seeds of fear. The fear paved the way for the entrance of, not only food allergies, but also air-born allergies.

After receiving ministry, including the healing of the trauma of abandonment, all her allergies went away overnight, almost instantly. Today she can share a bag of popcorn with me or eat corn chips and guacamole without any negative reaction - praise God!

3. Divorce is another horrendous trauma maker. Marriage is a covenant relationship and there is no pleasant way to end it. The husband and wife are hurt, the children are hurt, the grandparents are hurt, and friends are hurt. My dad left my mom when I was around two years old. Shortly after her divorce my mom remarried

and I grew up with my mother and step-dad. My mother had two children with her first husband, me with her second husband, and four children with her third husband. This all happened in the day when divorce was extremely rare. None of my classmates lived in such an environment. One day one of my friends came over to our house and he made an observation. He said, "Your two older sisters have the last name of Given, your last name is Frye, and your younger brothers and sisters have the name of Lawson. How come you're the only one named Frye?" I felt shame. I felt I was different in the sense that I didn't fit in. Divorce represents one of the greatest wound makers in our society.

4. Abuse

   a. Physical Abuse. I was on staff at Metro Church of Garland, TX, over the discipleship ministry, and enjoying myself immensely. The staff was fun to work with and the congregation was hungry to grow in the Lord. After I had been there about a year the senior pastor approached me one day saying that their mission church in Allen, TX was about to go belly-up. He asked if I would go there and try to salvage the fledgling church. I agreed to go but first I wanted to form a team from the mother church to go with me.

   I asked some dear friends of mine to join our team. John (not his real name) said, "Roger, we would love to go but..." Then he proceeded to describe the trauma his wife, Georgia (not her real name), went through in the city of Allen. They owned several rental properties in Allen and one day they were fixing up and cleaning one of their properties, getting it ready for a new renter. Georgia, wearing her grubby work clothes was out in the front yard dragging some tree cuttings toward the street for trash pickup. About that time a patrol car drove by and stopped. They began to accuse Georgia of crimes which she vehemently denied. They didn't believe her and began to physically rough her up. They handcuffed her, put her in the squad car hauled her off to jail.

Georgia, possessing a very sensitive nature experienced extreme trauma at the hands of these police officers. They later sued the City of Allen and won in a court of law so I know they were not exaggerating. Because of the trauma, Georgia could not step foot inside the city limits of Allen without having a major panic attack. In fact, just driving through the city led to an emotional meltdown, so I asked them if it would be okay for me to minister to her. They agreed so we found a private place in the church where I let her describe the events of that eventful day and to express her feelings. I led her to forgive those policemen. Then I said, "We know that Jesus lives in timelessness, right?" And she agreed. I continued, "We also know that He is omnipresent, right?" And she agreed to that statement as well. So I went on to say, "If those assertions are true then it would be impossible for Him not to have been there." And again she agreed. I instructed her to close her eyes and go back to that scene where the abuse took place. I asked, "Are you there?" And she answered yes. Then I coached her to use the eyes of her spirit to tell me where Jesus was in that scene. In amazement she exclaimed, "I see Him, He's standing right there with His arm around me." I asked, "Do you see His face?" "Yes," she answered. "What does He seem to be communicating just by His facial expression?" She said, "Deep compassion and pain for what is happening to me." "How does that feel?" She responded, "Wonderful! It's so comforting to see Him there with me." I asked the Lord to pull up all the pain, all the trauma of that event up out of her heart and we could both feel it lift out. Then I asked the Lord to put His hand on her heart and release His healing anointing.

I ministered to Georgia for about a half hour. From that day on, about 17 years ago, she has never experienced another panic attack while in the city of Allen. They went with us and served in that mission church until John retired and they moved out of the state. Not all trauma is healed that quickly but sometimes it is. Later, one of the staff members with a masters degree in counseling approached me at church declaring with excitement, "Roger, that was a miracle!" Yes, it was indeed a miracle but remember, our Lord is still in the business of mending broken hearts.

b. Spousal abuse.

Typically spousal abuse is seen as the man abusing the woman but it can be the other way around. Spousal abuse may be physical and it may be verbal or both. Emotional or mental abuse is still abuse. Spouses who are angry, domineering, controlling and use destructive words cause deep trauma in their mate.

c. Child abuse.

Children need proper discipline that is age appropriate in order to provide guidance and protection. Children need healthy boundaries to feel secure but don't confuse abuse with proper discipline. My step-dad corrected us kids out of anger, with screaming and yelling, pounding his fists on the table. When we correct our children out of anger we can break their spirit and they become discouraged. In Colossians 3:21 we are warned, *Fathers, do not provoke your children, lest they become discouraged.* The word "provoke" contains the connotation of irritating, stirring up, and exasperating. Angry, destructive, and caustic words cause deep pain in a child, breaking their spirit. Someone has said, "Children are like horses, they need to be trained but not broken."

When my step-dad corrected me and my siblings out of anger I hated it. I judged him for it and in my heart I made an inner vow that I would never treat my children that way. When I got married and had children, much to my dismay, I began to correct my children out of anger but I was blinded to my sin. After experiencing spiritual renewal I discovered that I could walk in sweet, sweet fellowship with God. I learned that I could not only talk to God but that He wanted to talk to me and I could hear His voice intuitively in my heart. It was wonderful! I looked forward to my daily quiet time with God in the morning when I would commune with Him.

One morning I went to my quiet place to pray and fellowship with the Lord and as I prayed I could not feel God's presence. It seemed that my prayers got no higher than the ceiling and my quiet time was empty and meaningless. Finally, after numerous attempts to reach God, I cried out in desperation, "God, what's wrong? Have I sinned?" And the Lord answered me and said, "You corrected your son out of anger yesterday and I want you to go get it right with him." I argued with God, "I can't go ask for forgiveness and tell him I was wrong. He's the son and I'm the dad. He will lose all respect for me." God was silent and I still couldn't get through and into the glory zone. I realized it was useless to try to argue with God. So I went to my son, who was about six or seven at the time. I knelt down in front of him and said, "Son, yesterday I corrected you out of anger and God has shown me how wrong that was. Will you forgive me?" A big smile came on his face and he said, "I forgive you dad." Then he reached out to hug me.

I went back to my prayer place and, to my delight, I entered into the glory, the manifest presence of God. It was awesome! But the next morning I got up and tried to pray and it was the same experience all over again. I couldn't get through. The heavens were brass. So finally I cried out, "God, what's wrong? What have I done?" And the Lord said, "You corrected your daughter yesterday out of anger and I want you to go get it right." I argued with God and complained, "Lord, if I confess my sin to her and ask for forgiveness she will lose all respect for me as her father." Again the Lord was silent. So reluctantly I went into the other room and found my daughter and kneeling down in front of her I said, "Heather, I corrected you out of anger yesterday and God has shown me how wrong that was. Will you forgive me?" She smiled and said, "I forgive you dad." And she gave me a big hug.

I went back to my place of prayer and easily moved into that place of intimate communion with God. You would think I would have learned my lesson in those two days but the same scenario repeated itself every day for what seemed to be 100 days. Finally I learned to correct my children using Godly wisdom rather that anger. Looking back I realize that my behavior would have changed so much more rapidly had I known the truth about judgments and inner vows.

d. Sexual abuse.

- Molestation. They tell us that three out of four women will be molested by the time they reach 16.

- Rape. Don't believe the lie that it was your fault you were raped. Rape is not about sex, it is about power and anger.

- Incest. Inappropriate touch or sexual relations between family members is strictly forbidden in Scripture. For example, Leviticus 18:8-18 (NIV) states, *Do not have sexual relations with your father's wife; that would dishonor your father. Do not have sexual relations with your sister, either your father's daughter or your mother's daughter, whether she was born in the same home or elsewhere. Do not have sexual relations with your son's daughter or your daughter's daughter; that would dishonor you. Do not have sexual relations with the daughter of your father's wife, born to your father; she is your sister. Do not have sexual relations with your father's sister; she is your father's close relative. Do not have sexual relations with your mother's sister, because she is your mother's close relative. Do not dishonor your father's brother by approaching his wife to have sexual relations; she is your aunt. Do not have sexual relations with your daughter-in-law. She is your son's wife; do not have relations with her. Do not have sexual relations with your brother's wife; that would dishonor your brother. Do not have sexual relations with both a woman and her daughter. Do not have sexual relations with either her son's daughter or her daughter's daughter; they are her close relatives. That is wickedness.*

- Exposure to sexual activity. For example, if a boy sees his mother in bed with a man who is not his daddy it creates deep trauma in him. Or, if he finds dad's pornographic material it defiles his spirit.

5. Death of a loved one or close friend.

When I was a kid my younger sister had a very close friend named Leslie and they hung out together all the time because they loved each other's company. One day little eight- year-old Leslie was riding her bicycle in the neighborhood when a young man, driving a pickup truck, doing 50 miles per hour in a 25 mile per hour zone, recklessly sped down the same road. He struck Leslie, killing her instantly. My sister went into shock and expressed no emotions for weeks. Ignorantly, people would chide her saying, "Why aren't you crying? How could you be so cold? What's wrong with you?" Their harsh words added trauma to her already traumatized heart.

6. Violence

I have a friend whose son was on fire for Christ. He often witnessed to people he met, went to church every time the doors were opened, loved to study his Bible and very enthusiastically and joyfully served the Lord. Then one day he was walking through the park in broad daylight where he was met by a group of very large, aggressive young men. They mercilessly beat him up and mugged him.

After that incident he lost his joy. The enthusiasm and the desire for corporate worship and Bible study left him. He had no desire to serve the Lord. What happened to cause such a drastic change for the worse in this young man's life? Trauma. He had to forgive, of course, but forgiveness is only one part of the equation. He needed his heart to be healed of the emotional trauma. The inner wounds provided an opening for the enemy to get in and torment his life.

Trap Number Seven: Trauma

We live in a violent culture where we witness horrific events on TV on a daily basis. Small children, who cannot separate fantasy from reality, receive great internal wounding by watching age-inappropriate television or movies. Some neighborhoods are rife with gang wars and drive-by shootings and stabbings, all of which create deep trauma. Schools conduct drills so students will know what to do in case a gunman comes in.

Soldiers and police officers often experience Post Traumatic Stress Disorder (PTSD) through the violence they encounter. However, PTSD is not limited to soldiers and police officers. Many civilians have developed this disorder through much trauma. I like what Dr. Michael Hutching says about this disorder and I'm going to paraphrase his teaching and use his prayer.

PTSD is a real-life medical diagnosed condition that primarily was first diagnosed as an anxiety disorder. It can develop **first** of all when a person experiences, witnesses, or is confronted with an event or events that involve actual, or threatened death, or serious injury, or threat to the physical integrity of one's self, or of another. Through these types of experiences they can suffer from this disorder. You can develop PTSD from something that was done to you but you can also experience it by just witnessing something that was done to another person.

A second factor that leads to PTSD is that the person's response involves intense fear, helplessness or horror. Their traumatic event is persistently re-experienced in one or more of the following ways. a) They experience recurrent and intrusive memories of the traumatic event. These memories include images, thoughts or perceptions. b) They experience recurring or distressing dreams or nightmares of the event. c) They act or feel as if the traumatic event is recurring. This includes reliving the experience, hallucinations, and flashback episodes. Many times those who have been involved in some kind of violent event, have dreams, nightmares, and/or night terrors about the event and they sometimes wake up engaged in the violent event.

Many PTSD victims, especially soldiers, cannot sleep with their spouses because there has been an incident where they woke up and tried to attack their spouse thinking that they're in the midst of a battle. d) They experience intense emotional distress when exposed to cues or triggers that cause them to re-live the traumatic event. Many individuals with PTSD also have a social anxiety disorder. They don't go where there are crowds of people. In fact they rarely go into public places. If they do happen to go into a public place they never sit with their back to the door. They are always on guard for threats, especially those that are veterans or war or active duty soldiers.

A third factor that points to PTSD is a persistent avoidance of the stimuli related to the trauma and a numbing of usual responsiveness. They begin to sense that they are not going to live much longer. They often have suicidal thoughts. Their sleep becomes constantly disrupted. They often experience difficulty falling or staying asleep. They become hyper-vigilant and this hyper-vigilance affects their body.

It is common for them to develop chronic nerve pain or myalgia. The hyper-vigilance over time destroys the nerves. Men with PTSD commonly hate to admit they have PTSD because to do so is to admit weakness. To admit weakness can be a humiliating thing for a veteran. PTSD patients are basically told that they will have to learn to cope with this disorder because there is no cure. Doctors prescribe medicines to help manage the situation but the problem is these medicines eventually lose their effectiveness. The body has a way of bringing itself to a toleration level so that the drug is no longer effective. Consequently they have to keep constantly switching meds and the meds often have many negative side effects. And often the medications work against themselves. These patients typically see themselves as a huge burden to their families and many of them contemplate suicide.

The good news, however, is that Jesus is still in the business of healing the traumas of our heart. There is no pain too difficult for Him to heal. Nevertheless, we still have to choose to let Jesus heal us. Most of our traumas and heartaches come not because we did something wrong. It's not our fault that we were raped, molested, mugged or robbed. We didn't do anything to invite them or tempt them to treat us badly. We didn't choose the traumatic events but we can choose how we deal with them. We can remain a victim or we can choose to rise up in the power of Christ and become a victor. When you develop a victim mindset you define yourself as a victim. A victim mindset means that you have received the rejection, shame, guilt, false responsibility and condemnation upon yourself and you define yourself according to the abuse done to you.

Not everyone is afflicted with this condition but there are a lot more Christians who are suffering from this disorder than we realize. I want everyone to receive this ministry so as not to single anyone out and embarrass them. Everyone please stand and look me in the eyes. The eyes are the window of the soul and I want to declare some things to your inner man, your spirit.

"In the name of Jesus Christ, I declare over you by the power of His blood that all shame is broken off of your life right now, in Jesus' Name, that you are no longer defined by your experience of others, your experience with yourself or any other traumatic event or any recurring pattern that has happened in your life. I break shame off of you, in Jesus' Name."

"No matter what you have done, if you ask the Father to release you of that, forgiveness is yours, in Jesus' Name. And I break off all guilt and responsibility and condemnation for anything that you've done, anything you've witnessed. I declare over you Romans 8:1, There is therefore now no condemnation for those who are in Christ. You are no longer defined by the history of what you've done because you are a new creation in Christ. That's the truth of God's Word."

"By the power of the blood of Jesus Christ I declare over you that you are not responsible for the abuse that you suffered. You are not responsible for that which injured your body and

soul. In the Name of Jesus I cleanse you from that right now in the Name of Jesus. I declare you are no longer defined by your history. What people have done to you does not declare who you are, in Jesus' Name."

"In the Name of Jesus, by the power of the blood of Jesus Christ I bring healing into your heart. I bind up your broken heart that you've carried for years and I break the power of fear and speak healing to the wound of fear. I break the power of anxiety and terror and I speak healing to anxiety and terror, in Jesus' Name. I break the power of abuse and I speak healing."

"Spirit of fear, I cast you away from them, in the Name of Jesus. Spirit of anxiety, I cast you away, in the Name of Jesus. Spirit of suicide, I cast you away, in the Name of Jesus. Spirit of trauma, I cast you away, in the Name of Jesus. Every afflicting spirit I cast you away from them, in the Name of Jesus. I break off of you the self-diagnosis that you are going crazy because you are not going crazy, you are tormented, you're wounded and you need healing, in Jesus' Name."

"I break off the lie that God is not going to protect you, in Jesus' Name. I break off the lie that God is punishing you, in Jesus' Name. I break off the lie that you're going to have to live with this the rest of your life."

"In Jesus' Name I speak faith, trust, peace and the promise of protection over you according to Psalm 91. I take authority over all pathways, portals or means of access or connection that allow tormenting spirits to bring fear, anxiety, worry, paranoia, nightmares, night terrors and traumatic memories and images, in Jesus' Name."

"In Jesus' Name I cancel every assignment of the powers of darkness and tormenting spirits against their spirit, mind and body. I command all afflicting and tormenting spirits to leave and never return, in Jesus' Name. I declare healing of the mind, the nervous system, the lymphatic system, the muscular system (that deals with muscle memory) and any physical wound or injury that is connected to the traumatic events."

"I disconnect the triggers of the five senses that bring back memory. Seeing, be disconnected from traumatic images or ideas, in Jesus' Name. Hearing, I disconnect you from traumatic sounds, in Jesus' Name. Tasting, I disconnect you from traumatic memories, in Jesus' Name. Feeling, I disconnect you from the physical pain of traumatic events, in Jesus' Name. Smelling, I disconnect you from traumatic memories, in Jesus' Name. I disconnect the five senses as being triggers to past traumatic events.

"In the Name of Jesus, whatever you have done to harm anyone, whatever you have done that is in any way shape or form harmful, the power of the blood of Jesus Christ has forgiven you and set you free and I'm declaring release from prison. You are no longer in prison. The shackles and chains are broken off of you and you're free, in the Name of Jesus."

"In Jesus Name, I declare Isaiah 61 over you. I declare liberty to the captive and I declare release to the prisoner. You no longer have to serve punishment time for what you have done. I declare freedom to you mind, to your body, and to your spirit, in Jesus' Name."

"Holy Spirit, I ask You to bring reintegration to _____'s brain and restore healthy connections between _____'s soul, spirit and body. Holy Spirit, I ask You to heal the brain to such an extent that the left and right brain are connected again and that _____ can begin to function in such a way that he/she has freedom, in Jesus' Name." (These declarations were developed by Dr. Mike Hutchings and adapted by Roger Frye. See endnotes.)

Please repeat this declaration after me.

I am a new creation in Christ, the old is passed away, all things have become new. I am in Jesus, Jesus is in me. Greater is He who

is in me, than He who is in the world. I'm loved. I'm forgiven. I'm kept by His blood. I'm accepted, by a loving Father, who loves me, no matter what. In Jesus' Name, I am seated with Christ, in heavenly places. I am His workmanship, created to do good works, for His glory. I am more that a conqueror, through Him who loves me. I am no longer a victim, but I am a victor. I am an overcomer, in Jesus' Name. Everything in my life that is good, comes from the Father. Therefore, all things, work together for my good, because I love God, and I'm called according to His purpose. I have an assignment, I'm going to heaven. In the meantime, I have an assignment here, I'm bringing heaven to earth. I carry the power of God, by Jesus, and Holy Spirit, the very same Spirit, that raised Jesus from the dead, lives in me. Therefore, I have no fear. God has not given me a spirit of fear, but of power, love, and a sound mind, in Jesus' Name. (Now spend some time thanking and praising God.) [11]

Painful, negative experiences cause our hearts to become fertile soil in which the enemy can sow lies - lies about God, ourselves and others. As mature Christians we would never believe these lies in our head but down at the heart level the lies have been implanted. When the rubber meets the road, when we face the challenges and trials of everyday life, what is in our heart is going to come out. We usually react to the vicissitudes of life out of what is in our hearts, not out of what information we hold in our heads. The lies themselves create more pain and the pain doesn't just go away as the years go by. These lies hold us in captivity. To get free we must deal with the lies head on. Jesus said, *You shall know the truth and the truth shall set you free* (John 8:32). The lies must be exposed, confessed, and renounced. Then ask God for His corresponding truth because the truth will make you free.

7. Betrayal

Betrayal is a huge wound maker. Some examples of betrayal include: 1) you catch your husband or wife in bed with your best friend, 2) a close friend at work goes behind your back to manipulate the boss in order to get your position, 3) a trusted

Trap Number Seven: Trauma

friend goes around talking about something that you shared in confidence. To betray someone means to be disloyal. Let me tell you a story of betrayal from my own life.

I accepted a call from a church to be their new senior pastor. Things went quite well for the first several months. We saw people saved every Sunday and rarely did a week go by without a baptismal service. Then one day the deacons approached me and said, "Pastor, we want you to stop preaching salvation messages because people are getting tired of it." I explained that I had not been preaching "salvation messages" and that I had been preaching the Lordship of Christ messages but in the process of it people were getting saved. They said, "Whatever you call it, we need you to stop or you will lose half the church." So I decided to tone down the messages a bit until the people adjusted to their new pastor and then I would start diving in again to the meat of God's Word.

When I toned the sermons down the deacons commented, "Well, if you could change your style of preaching it means that you weren't sincere in the first place." It was a no win situation. Things went from bad to worse as I was constantly undergoing attacks from disgruntled church members and as I feverishly worked to put out fires on a weekly or even daily basis.

Then one day a business man in the church approached me and said, "Pastor, what you need is a friend- someone you can unload your burdens to. Why don't we start meeting once a week for breakfast and you can talk to me about anything that's on your heart. I want to be your friend." His invitation sounded very good to me in light of the difficulties I was facing. We met every Friday morning at a local restaurant and it felt so good to have a trusted friend to confide in. Every week he listened attentively and seemed to be genuinely concerned. Then one Friday, after an especially hard week, I asked him, "What's wrong? Why are there so many problems in the church?" He looked at me in the eyes and said, "Pastor, you're the problem." He got up, walked out, and proceeded to raise up a coup against me.

I can't begin to express the depth of the pain his words and actions caused. My trusted friend betrayed me. Betrayal is the deepest and most destructive of the wounds we can encounter. Within a short period of time the church called for a special business meeting. I understand that the vote was close but the simple majority of the congregation decided to give me the "left foot of fellowship." When I received the news it felt like I had literally been kicked in the stomach by a mule. The devastating news made me physically ill.

After about a year or two my wife and I moved to Texas to be closer to our children who had made Texas their home. Shortly after that a growing church in Garland, Texas called me to be their pastor of discipleship. While in that capacity I came across a ministry that specialized in inner healing. One of the ministers in that organization helped me locate a lie that I had received as a result of my betrayal. The lie in my heart was, "You can't trust Christians." How many of you know that it's hard to be a pastor if you believe that lie in your heart?

The prayer minister led me to confess, renounce and break the power of that lie. That ministry proved very helpful in my healing process but God had more in store. In my own prayer time, as I quieted myself in God's presence, in a vision, God took me back to that restaurant scene where I was betrayed. As my "friend" said those hurtful words I saw Jesus standing beside me with one hand on my shoulder. With the other hand He reached over and pulled a long thorn out of my heart. The thorn was about three inches long and kind of curved like a deer antler. Then He reached down again putting His hand on my heart to heal the wound. It was amazing how healing this experience proved.

8. The absence of good things. The absence of good things or neglect represents the most difficult form of trauma to heal. The reason is that it's far easier to identify the bad things that happen to us. Small children often misbehave because they want attention. They would rather get negative attention than no attention at all. The deepest wounds come through indifference. Did your father

spend quality time with you as a child? Did he hold you in his lap and tell you he loved you? If not, you have what we call a "father wound." I was raised with six siblings and, with seven children, my mom was a little burned out. She would escape by reading for many hours and she often ignored the needs of her kids. Although she was a very kind and godly woman with many positive qualities, her disengagement from her children caused wounding. Many people suffer from what we call a "mother wound."

Jesus wants to heal the wounds of our hearts if we will just let him. Don't just stuff it down and pretend it's not there because the pain will come out in an unhealthy way.

How do we receive healing from traumatic, painful memories? Remember that God truly cares about every painful event in your life. In the New Testament Jesus was always gentle and compassionate with those who were hurting. When we come to God for healing of our inner wounds He never rebukes us or chides us. He never says, "Shame on you. It's your fault. You brought it on yourself. You should have been more diligent." No. He is our loving Father who hurts when we hurt and He wants us healed.

The Bible states in Matthew 12:20-22 that, *A bruised reed He will not break, and smoking flax He will not quench, till He sends forth justice to victory; and in His name Gentiles will trust.*

In Biblical days shepherds would stay out in the hills away from people to tend their sheep and lead them to water and fresh pastures. Having a lot of spare time on their hands they would take a reed and cut it to make a little musical instrument and entertain themselves with their music. But in the course of everyday events in the life of a shepherd they would often bruise the reed by accidently stepping on it or leaning against something as it hung at their waist, thus distorting the sound quality. Rather than attempting to repair it, they would break up the damaged reed and find another reed to make a new musical instrument.

God is saying that He doesn't treat His children that way. When we get bruised by the trials of life so that we cannot function the way we were created He doesn't just discard us. He doesn't cast us away and start all over with someone else. He patiently and gently works to repair us so that we can operate according to our original design.

The Lord uses another analogy to show us His steadfast love. In ancient times oil lamps were used to provide light. A wick was placed in a bowl of oil with the top part resting inside a little lip. After the wick absorbed the oil it was lit to provide light. After burning for an extended period the wick would start to emit an inordinate amount of smoke becoming annoying to the home owner. Then the person would reach down and pinch off the burnt tip of the wick and relight it. God is saying that He doesn't treat His children like that. If we start "smoking" instead of emitting light according to our original design, He doesn't reach down and extinguish us. Rather, He fans the flame and rekindles the fire.

God doesn't turn His back on us just because our heart is broken. Notice what He says in Psalm 34:18, *The LORD is near to those who have a broken heart, and saves such as have a contrite spirit.*

To be healed of our trauma we need to have a personal revelation of God's love. Simply reading about it in the Bible will not suffice unless that passage of Scripture comes alive in our heart. Ephesians 1:6 represents an example of a great verse on the love of God where it states, *to the praise of the glory of His grace, by which He made us accepted in the Beloved.* We can read and memorize this verse, hear sermons on this passage, teach it to our Bible study group but unless those words come alive in our heart they are just letters on a page that sound good. We may know about God's love intellectually but God wants us to know His love experientially.

Years ago I pastored a church in Northern California. One day Sherry (not her real name), a member of our church, called our home. In an extremely animated voice she excitedly declared, "Pastor, pastor, something wonderful has happened to me and

I'm excited!" My curiosity aroused I asked, "Sherry, what is it?" She said, "It's too wonderful, too life changing to tell you over the phone." I encouraged her to come to our home immediately to which she enthusiastically agreed. She came to the door and I welcomed her in. Her face was beaming and she almost danced with excitement.

I asked, "Sherry, what is it? Tell me." Ruthie and I couldn't wait to hear what she had to say. So she exclaimed, "God loves me!" I replied, "Sherry, yes, that's good, but what else?" She said, "Pastor, you don't understand. God loves me, God loves me." By this time she was jumping up and down. She continued, "I've been active in the church all my life, I've sung in the choir, taught Sunday School, but for the first time in my life I really understand, God showed me, that He loves me. He loves me personally." I'll never get over the excitement and joy I saw in her face that day. What happened to Sherry was that she received a personal revelation of God's love and it was life changing. When we receive a personal revelation of God's immense, unending love, when we truly get a glimpse of God's love, His love has a way of healing the traumas of our life.

Once we have forgiven those who hurt us and we have received God's love, we must let go of the hurts. God is able to take care of those who hurt us so we need to let go and release them into God's hands and let go of the hurt. God is able to cause good to come from the pain we've endured. In Romans 8:28 we read, *And we know that all things work together for good to those who love God, to those who are the called according to His purpose.* I often say, "God is able to take our pain and make it our gain, He can take our test and make it our testimony, and He can take our mess and make it our message."

Sometimes we have to stop being self-focused and focus on serving others before God allows our healing to progress. It's like the Dead Sea. Nothing lives in the Dead Sea, it cannot support life. The reason is that this lake has no outlet. Water flows in but nothing flows out causing the salt and mineral content to rise too high to sustain life. Similarly, we need an outlet. We need to pour love into the lives of others in order to heal ourselves. That's the way God created us.

I pastored a church in North Texas and Janet, a member of the church, was one of the most needy persons I've ever known. Every week, either at Sunday morning worship or at the midweek care group, her life represented a maze of problems. Our people regularly ministered to her and were happy to do so but she was a living sponge. She would suck the energy out of you with her endless list of personal challenges.

Then one day the director of the children's department asked her if she would like to assist in that program. She accepted the invitation and wholeheartedly went to work pouring her energy into the lives of these kids. She sent post cards to the children that missed, she prepared art projects and lesson support materials, encouraged, and guided the students in class projects, and an amazing transformation took place in Janet. Her face seemed to exude peace. She quit talking about her host of problems and she expressed genuine content verbally and nonverbally. What happened? It was simple, she quit thinking about herself and concentrated on the lives of the children. God heals us so that we may be vessels through which God can heal others.

Jesus said it this way, *Give, and it will be given to you: good measure, pressed down, shaken together, and running over will be put into your bosom. For with the same measure that you use, it will be measured back to you*. This is God's law of sowing and reaping. If we sow love it will return to us, if we sow healing it will come back to us.

The main thing is that we release our hurts and pains to Jesus for Him to heal. Remember He said that He came to heal the broken hearted. When He died on the cross He made provision for all our rejection, shame, and woundedness to be healed. Listen to the words of Isaiah as he prophesied of the coming Messiah.

He is despised and rejected by men, a Man of sorrows and

Trap Number Seven: Trauma

acquainted with grief. And we hid, as it were, our faces from Him; He was despised, and we did not esteem Him. Surely He has borne our griefs and carried our sorrows; yet we esteemed Him stricken, smitten by God, and afflicted. But He was wounded for our transgressions, He was bruised for our iniquities; the chastisement for our peace was upon Him, and by His stripes we are healed. All we like sheep have gone astray; we have turned, every one, to his own way; and the LORD has laid on Him the iniquity of us all (Isaiah 53:3-6).

Prayer

Now put your hand on your heart and open up your heart as best as you can. If you are accustomed to hiding your feelings by pushing them down, I give you permission to get in touch with your pain as we pray.

"Lord Jesus, You said You came to heal the broken hearted so I ask that You come and heal our hearts today. Lord, You said that, *Peace I leave with you, My peace I give to you; not as the world gives do I give to you. Let not your heart be troubled, neither let it be afraid* (John 14:27). So I ask that You release Your peace in us, the peace that passes understanding. Let's soak up His peace for a moment. Breathe in the peace from the One who is called The Prince of Peace. Now let's take a moment to soak up His love knowing that the Bible says that God is love."

"In the mighty name of Jesus Christ of Nazareth I bind any spirit of trauma that was sent to lock in the trauma in your life. I praise You Lord that You did not give us a spirit of fear but of power and of love and of a sound mind."

"I ask, Heavenly Father, that You would wash over us with the Living Water of Your Presence and cleanse us of all pain, trauma, defilement, shame, and guilt. Pull up all the pain of abandonment, betrayal, abuse, neglect, divorce, accidents, violence, and the death of a loved one. Lord Jesus, You suffered and died for us and by faith we appropriate Your finished work on the cross and Your resurrection."

"Heavenly Father, we confess the sins of those in our generations past who traumatized manipulated, controlled, or dominated others. Heal all the trauma that was passed on to us through our generations. Heal our DNA and cleanse it of all trauma, shame, fear, and horror and bring our DNA back into Your original design."

"Holy Spirit, please release Your love, joy, and peace into the cells of our body that have stored any trauma and restore those cells to their original design. Bring your healing power to every area where our heart has been broken. Fill every cell with You peace and grace."

"Jesus, pull up the pain that has been pushed way down deep inside. Put Your hand on our hearts and release Your healing anointing, in Jesus' Name, Amen."

CHAPTER NINE

Freedom From Evil Spirits

The Bible references evil spirits around 115 times, calling them demons, foul spirits, and once, an unclean spirit. The average church today does not wish to delve into the subject of demonology, and understandably so, for fear of offending someone or out of concern that the subject be taken to an extreme by some over-zealous members. However, the Bible unashamedly speaks of evil spirits because they really exist.

We don't have to fear evil spirits because the Bible states, *You are of God, little children, and have overcome them, because He who is in you is greater than he who is in the world* (1 John 4:4). The Holy Spirit indwells all believers and the Holy Spirit possesses infinitely more power than the devil and all his minions. When we thoroughly deal with the seven traps these spirits lose their hold on the believer but they may still be present.

A Christian cannot be possessed by an evil spirit because the word "possessed" implies ownership. God owns believers and the Bible says that we are bought with a price. Unfortunately, the modern translations usually get this wrong. The word "possessed" is never used of demonic activity in the original Greek language of the New Testament. In most cases the best translation would be "demonized." "Demonized" implies influence. Christians can be influenced by evil spirits; some people are more influenced than others. In other passages of Scripture the original language simply means, "to have a demon" but never does it mean "owned," or "possessed."

These demonic spirits gain a foothold through the Christian falling into one or more of the seven traps. They are sent to attempt to keep the Christian in bondage through lies, deceit, and intimidation. Once you receive ministry and get freed from the seven traps it behooves you to oust any evil spirits that may be present.

Sixteen different times the Bible says, "the spirit of" in reference to an evil spirit. There are other references where it says, "the Spirit of" when referring to the Holy Spirit. I'm convinced that there are 16 distinct demonic spirits named in the Bible and when you look at the context of these passages you will discover the corresponding sins that hold them in place. It makes it much easier for them to leave and to stay away if you confess and repent of the corresponding sins.

We start by confessing the sins of our fathers (ancestors). People in our generational line may have committed sins related to these root spirits that brought iniquity into our lives which hinders our ability to obtain freedom. According to Scripture, iniquity gets passed on to the third and fourth generation. *For I the LORD your God, am a jealous God, visiting the iniquity of the fathers on the children to the third and fourth generations of those who hate Me* (Exodus 20:5, NKJV). Children suffer from the sins of their fathers. After David sinned with Bathsheba, 2 Samuel 12:19 says, *When David saw that his servants were whispering, David perceived that the child was dead. Therefore David said to his servants, "Is the child dead?" And they said, "He is dead."* The child suffered death because of the sins of his parents.

Iniquity brought into our bloodline by the sins of our ancestors actually puts a curse on our ability to walk the path of freedom. The good news, however, is that it is fairly easy to break these curses, thus bringing the freedom God intends us to have.

Scripture contains references about confessing the sins of our ancestors. Daniel confessed the sins of his fathers as well as the sins of the nation (Dan. 9:3-17). Nehemiah also confessed the sins of his fathers. Both my father's house and I have sinned. We have acted very corruptly against You, and have not kept the commandments, the statutes, the ordinances which You have commanded Your servant Moses (Neh. 1:6c-7). The Israelites confessed the sins of their fathers. Then those of Israelite lineage separated themselves from all foreigners; and they stood and confessed their sins and the iniquities of their fathers (Nehemiah 9:2).

Let me relate this concept to your ability to walk out your freedom. Sins that your ancestors committed can pass on iniquity to you that gives you a propensity to get stuck by the schemes of the enemy. But be of good courage. You don't have to stay in bondage to the sins of our forefathers. Through confession and renunciation we can break the hold of any iniquity that we've inherited. We will start by confessing and renouncing the sins of our ancestors and renouncing any corresponding conditions. Let's deal decisively with the 16 root spirits.

Prayers of Confession and Repentance

1. Numbers 5:14

*If **the spirit of jealousy** comes upon him and he becomes jealous of his wife, who has defiled herself; or if **the spirit of jealousy** comes upon him and he becomes jealous of his wife, although she has not defiled herself—*

Say this out loud, "I confess and renounce the sin of envy, covetousness, resentment, suspicion, distrust, anger, wrath, rage, wishing a person was dead, and the tendency to be easily offended, in the lives of my generations past." Now go back over the list of sins and say, "I confess and repent of my sin of _____ ." (Name all sins related to the spirit of jealousy that you have personally committed.)

Next, address the evil spirit, knowing, that as a believer, you have the authority to do so. Say, "Spirit of jealousy, I reject you, I renounce you, and I break any agreements I've ever made with you and I command you to bow the knee to the Lord Jesus Christ, leave me now, and go to dry places, in Jesus' Name." Jesus taught that when a spirit goes out of a person it goes through dry places seeking rest (Matthew 12:43) so this is a legitimate way to deal with them. Other prayer ministers choose to send them to the feet of Jesus for Him to dispose of as He sees fit. I believe either approach is optional. It seems that most people need a prayer minister to come alongside and help them in this process, especially if this concept is new to them. Keep in mind that commonly individuals yawn during this exercise. If you feel like you need to yawn, go ahead and yawn. It is not communicating boredom. In fact it may prove helpful to take a deep breath through your nose and from your diaphragm and then exhale through your mouth after you have commanded the spirit to leave.

2. Judges 9:23

*God sent a **spirit of ill will** between Abimelech and the men of Shechem; and the men of Shechem dealt treacherously with Abimelech.*

Say this out loud, "I confess and renounce the sin of murder, jockeying for position, divisiveness, contention, animosity, hostility, hatred, bitterness, unpleasantness, resentment, and unfriendliness in the lives of my generations past." Now go back over the list of sins and say, "I confess and repent of my sin of _____." (Name all sins related to the spirit of ill will that you have personally committed.) Remember, that for New Testament believers, murder includes the attitude of the heart. To be so angry you wish a person was dead is tantamount to murder in the eyes of God.

Next, address the spirit of ill will saying, "Spirit of ill will, I reject you, I renounce you, I break all agreements I ever made with you and I command you to leave me now and go to dry places, in Jesus' Name."

3. 2 Chronicles 18:21

So he said, "I will go out and be a lying spirit in the mouth of all his prophets." And the LORD said, "You shall persuade him and also prevail; go out and do so."

Say this out loud, "I confess and renounce the sin of deceit, dishonesty, lying, insincerity, hypocrisy, double standards, two-facedness, and flattery in the lives of my generations past." Now go back over the list of sins and say, "I confess and repent of my sin of _____." (Name all sins related to the spirit of lying that you have personally committed.)

Next, address the spirit of lying saying, "Spirit of lying, I reject you, I renounce you, I break all agreements I ever made with you and I command you to leave me now and go to dry places, in Jesus' Name.

4. Proverbs 16:18

*Pride goes before destruction, and a **haughty spirit** before a fall.*

Say this out loud, "I confess and renounce the sin of pride, arrogance, false humility, conceit, superiority, mockery, self-importance, and over-confidence in the live of my generations past." Now go back over the list of sins and say, "I confess and repent of my sin of _____." (Name all sins related to the spirit of haughtiness that you have personally committed.)

Next, address the haughty spirit saying, "Spirit of haughtiness, I reject you, I renounce you, I break all agreements I ever made with you and I command you to leave me now and go to dry places, in Jesus' Name."

5. Isaiah 29:10

*For the LORD has poured out on you the **spirit of deep sleep**, And has closed your eyes, namely, the prophets; and He has covered your heads, namely, the seers.*

Say this out loud, "I confess and renounce the sin of relying on human wisdom, disobedience, spiritual blindness, and honoring God with words while the heart is far from Him in the lives of my generations past." Now go back over the list of sins and say, "I confess and repent of my sin of _____." (Name all sins related to the spirit of deep sleep that you have personally committed.)

Next, address the spirit of deep sleep saying, "Spirit of deep sleep, I reject you, I renounce you, I break all agreements I ever made with you and I command you to leave me now and go to dry places, in Jesus' Name."

6. Isaiah 61:3

*To console those who mourn in Zion, to give them beauty for ashes, The oil of joy for mourning, the garment of praise for the **spirit of heaviness;** that they may be called trees of righteousness, the planting of the LORD, that He may be glorified.*

Say this out loud, "I confess and renounce the sin of self-pity, giving into the victim spirit, and listening to shame in the lives of my generations past." Now go back over the list of sins and say, "I confess and repent of my sin of _____ ." (Name all sins related to the spirit of heaviness that you have personally committed.)

Then say," I reject and renounce any depression, despair, discouragement, unjustified guilt, shame, false responsibility, loneliness, defilement, and hopelessness in me and in my bloodline, in Jesus' Name."

Next, address the spirit of heaviness saying, "Spirit of heaviness, I reject you, I renounce you, I break all agreements I ever made with you and I command you to leave me now and go to dry places, in Jesus' Name."

7. Hosea 4:12

*My people ask counsel from their wooden idols, And their staff informs them. For the **spirit of harlotry** has caused them to stray, And they have played the harlot against their God.*

Say this out loud, "I confess and renounce the sin of idolatry, sex outside of marriage, pornography, bestiality, compulsive masturbation, sexual fantasies, lust, and objectifying a woman/man in the lives of my generations past." Now go back over the list of sins and say, "I confess and repent of my sin of _____ ." (Name all sins related to the spirit of harlotry that you have personally committed.)

Next, address the spirit of harlotry saying, "Spirit of harlotry, I reject you, I renounce you, I break all agreements I ever made with you and I command you to leave me now and go to dry places, in Jesus' Name."

8. Mark 9:25-27

When Jesus saw that the people came running together, He rebuked the unclean spirit, saying to it: **'Deaf and dumb spirit***, I command you, come out of him and enter him no more!' Then the spirit cried out, convulsed him greatly, and came out of him. And he became as one dead, so that many said, 'He is dead.' But Jesus took him by the hand and lifted him up, and he arose.*

Say this out loud, "I confess and renounce the sin of unbelief and occultism in the lives of my generations past." Now if you have ever entertained unbelief or occultism say, "I confess and repent of all unbelief and occultism in my life. Lord I believe but help my unbelief."

Then say, "I reject and renounce epilepsy, grinding of the teeth, seizures, convulsions, accidents involving water/fire, and diseases of the eyes, ears, nose and throat in my life and in the lives of my generations past."

Next, address the deaf and dumb spirit saying, "Deaf and dumb spirit, I reject you, I renounce you, and I break all agreements I ever made with you, and I command you to leave me now and go to dry places, in Jesus' Name."

9. Luke 13:11

And behold, there was a woman who had a **spirit of infirmity** *eighteen years, and was bent over and could in no way raise herself up.*

Say this, "I reject and renounce the spirit of infirmity and _____ (Name any specific diseases in you and in your direct bloodline.) in my life and in the lives of my generations past."

Next, say, "Spirit of infirmity, I reject you, I renounce you, I break any agreement I ever made with you and I command you to leave me now and go to dry places, in Jesus' Name, Amen."

10. Acts 16:16

*Now it happened, as we went to prayer, that a certain slave girl possessed with a **spirit of divination** met us, who brought her masters much profit by fortune-telling.*

Say this out loud, "I confess and renounce any involvement in astrology, channeling, crystal balls, eight balls, fortune telling, demonic games, horoscopes, rebellion, independence, hypnosis, Ouija boards, palm reading, Satanism, séances, tarot cards, manipulation, witchcraft, and Freemasonry in the lives of my generations past." Now go back over the list saying, "I confess and repent of my involvement in _____ ." (Name the specific occultic activities that you were personally involved in.)

Next, say, "Spirit of divination, I reject you, I renounce you, I break any agreement I ever made with you, and I command you to leave me now and go to dry places, in Jesus' Name."

11. Romans 11:8

*Just as it is written: "God has given them a **spirit of stupor**, Eyes that they should not see and ears that they should not hear, To this very day."*

Say this out loud, "I confess and renounce the sin of procrastination, self-pity, passivity, and not wanting to be born in the lives of my generations past." Now go back over the list of sins saying, "I confess and repent of my sin of _____ ." (Name the sins you personally committed.)

Then say, "I reject and renounce all constant fatigue, and drawing back from life in my life and in the lives of my generations past."

Next, say, "Spirit of stupor, I reject you, I renounce you, I break all agreements I ever made with you, and I command you to leave me now and go to dry places, in Jesus' Name."

12. Romans 8:15

*For you did not receive the **spirit of bondage** again to fear, but you received the Spirit of adoption by whom we cry out, "Abba, Father."*

Say this out loud, "I reject and renounce addictions to possessions, alcohol, cigarettes, a person (co-dependency), work, computers, drugs, food, TV, video games, sex and any other addictions in the lives of my generations past. Now go back over the list of addictions saying, "I confess and repent of my addiction to _____ ." (Fill in the blank.)

Now say, "I confess the benefit I get from these addictions and the sin of looking to them for comfort."

Next, say, "Spirit of bondage, I reject you, I renounce you, I break any agreement I ever made with you, and I command you to leave me now and go to dry places, in Jesus' Name.

13. 2 Timothy 1:7

*For God has not given us a **spirit of fear**, but of power and of love and of a sound mind.*

Since God commands us numerous times in His Word to fear not, then if we give into fear we are breaking His command and, therefore, we need to confess it as sin in order for it to loose its hold on us.

Say out loud, "I confess and renounce the sin of coming into agreement with the spirit of fear, including the fear of abandonment, anxiety, faithlessness, fright, inadequacy, inferiority, worry, performance orientation, phobias, rejection, self-rejection, shyness, tension/stress, timidity, torment, perfectionism, fear of death, fear of failure, fear of men/women, fear of poverty, fear of success, fear of authority, and fear of loss in the lives of my generations past. Now go back over the list of fears saying, "I confess and repent of my sin of coming into agreement with _____ ." (Name the fears you have come into agreement with.)

Next, say, "Spirit of fear, I reject you, I renounce you, I break all agreements ever made with you, and I command you to leave me now and go to dry places, in Jesus' Name."

14. 1 John 4:3

*And every spirit that does not confess that Jesus Christ has come in the flesh is not of God. And this is the **spirit of the Antichrist**, which you have heard was coming, and is now already in the world.*

Say out loud, "I confess and renounce the sin of blaspheming the Holy Spirit, having a religious spirit, causing a church split, speaking ill of other pastors, teachers and evangelists, opposing the Bible or certain passages, rationalizing the Word, opposing Christ's deity and humanity, and wanting to give up on Christianity in the lives of my generations past." Now go back over the list of sins related to the antichrist spirit saying, "I confess and repent of my sin of _____ ." (Name the sins you have personally committed.)

Next say, "Spirit of antichrist, I reject you, I renounce you, and I break all agreements I ever made with you and I command you to leave me now and go to dry places, in Jesus' Name."

15. 1 John 4:6

*We are of God. He who knows God hears us; he who is not of God does not hear us. By this we know the spirit of truth and the **spirit of error**.*

Say out loud, "I confess and renounce the sin of compromising convictions, of sitting under false teachers, doubt and unbelief, inappropriate thinking and behavior, and immaturity and I reject and renounce confusion in the lives of my generations past." Now go back over the list of sins related to the spirit of error say, "I confess and repent of my sin of _____." (Name the sins you have personally committed.)

If applicable say, "I renounce the corresponding condition of confusion in my life."

Next, say, "Spirit of error, I reject you, I renounce you, I break any agreements ever made with you and I command you to leave me now and go to dry places, in Jesus' Name."

16. Isaiah 19:14

*The LORD has mingled a **perverse spirit** in her midst; and they have caused Egypt to err in all her work, as a drunken man staggers in his vomit.*

Say out loud, "I confess and renounce the sin of adhering to false teachers and doctrine, participation in multi-partner orgies, involvement in sadomasochism and other sexual deviations, and legalism in the lives of my generations past. Now go back over the list of sins saying, "I confess and repent of my sin of _____." (Name the sins you have personally committed.)

Then say, "I renounce any gender confusion, distortion, confusion, and twisted thinking in my life and in the lives of my generations past."

Next, say, "Perverse spirit, I reject you, I renounce you, and I break all agreements I ever made with you and I command you to leave me now and go to dry places, in Jesus' Name."

Now that this junk has left you we need to fill up any vacated areas with the Holy Spirit. Please say this out loud, "Holy Spirit, I welcome You, I honor You, and I confess that I need You. I cannot live the Christian life in my own strength so I ask You to fill me now. Come and seal all that You have done in my life with Your presence and Your power, in Jesus' Name, Amen.

Now let's celebrate! Begin to thank and praise God for what He has done.

APPENDIX

Prayer Of Release For Masons And Their Descendants

Selwyn Stevens (Adapted by Karen Sackett)

If you or someone you love is a descendant of a Mason, I recommend that you pray through the following prayer from your heart. Don't be like the Masons who are given their obligations and oaths one line at a time and without prior knowledge of the requirements. First, bind spirits of deception, antichrist, witchcraft, and death in the name of Jesus Christ. Then read it through so you know what is involved. It is best to pray this aloud with a Christian witness or counselor present. We suggest a brief pause following each paragraph to allow the Holy Spirit to show any additional issues that may require attention.

Father God, creator of heaven and earth, I come to You in the name of Jesus Christ Your Son. I come as a sinner seeking forgiveness and cleansing from all sins committed against You, and others made in your image. I honor my earthly father and mother and all of my ancestors of flesh and blood and by adoption, but I utterly turn away from and renounce all their sins. I forgive all my ancestors for the effects of their sins on my children and me. I confess and renounce all of my own sins. I renounce Satan and all of his works in my family and me.

I renounce and forsake all involvement in Freemasonry or any other lodge or craft by my ancestors and myself. I renounce witchcraft, the principal spirit behind Freemasonry, and I renounce Baphomet, the Spirit of Antichrist and the curse of the Luciferian doctrine. I renounce the idolatry, blasphemy, secrecy, and deception of Masonry at every level. I specifically renounce the insecurity, the love of position and power, the love of money, covetousness, and greed, and the pride that would have led my ancestors into Masonry. I renounce all the fears that held them in Masonry, especially the fears of death, fears of men, and fears of trusting, in the name of Jesus Christ.

I renounce every position held in the lodge by any of my ancestors, including Tyler, Master, Worshipful Master, or any other. I renounce the calling of any man Master, for Jesus Christ is my only Master and Lord, and He forbids anyone else having that title. I renounce the entrapping of others into Masonry, and observing the helplessness of others during the rituals. I renounce the effects of Masonry passed on to me through any female ancestor who felt distrusted and rejected by her husband as he entered and attended any lodge and refused to tell her of his secret activities.

THE BLUE LODGE

First Degree: I renounce the oaths taken by any of my ancestors or me and the curses involved in the First or Entered Apprentice Degree, especially their effects on the throat and tongue. I renounce the Hoodwink, the blindfold, and its effects on emotions and eyes, including all confusion, fear of the dark, fear of the light, and fear of sudden noises. I renounce the secret word, BOAZ, and all it means. I renounce the mixing and mingling of truth and error, and the blasphemy of this degree of Masonry. I renounce the noose around the neck, the fear of choking and also every spirit causing asthma, hay fever, emphysema or any other breathing difficulty. I renounce the compass point, sword or spear held against the breast, the fear of death by stabbing pain and the fear of heart attack from this degree. In the name of Jesus Christ, I now pray for the healing of the throat, vocal cords, nasal passages, sinuses, bronchial tubes, allergies and asthma, for healing of the speech area, and the release of the word of God to me and through my family and me.

Second Degree: I renounce the oaths taken by any of my ancestors or me and the curses involved in the Second or Fellow Craft Degree of Masonry, especially the curses on the heart and chest. I renounce the secret words JACHIN and SHIBBOLETH and all that these mean. I cut off emotional hardness, apathy, indifference, unbelief, and deep anger from my family and me. In the name of Jesus Christ I pray for the healing of the chest/lung/heart area and for the healing of my emotions and ask to be made sensitive to the Holy Spirit of God.

Third Degree: I renounce the oaths taken by any of my ancestors or me and the curses involved in the Third or Master Mason Degree, especially the curses on the stomach and womb area. I renounce the secret words MAH-HAH-BONE, MACHABEN, MACHBINNA and TUBAL CAIN, and all that they mean. I renounce the spirit of death from the blows to the head enacted as ritual murder, the fear of death, false martyrdom, fear of violent gang attack, assault, or rape, and the helplessness of this degree. I renounce the falling into the coffin or stretcher involved in the ritual murder. I renounce the false resurrection of this degree, because only Jesus Christ is the Resurrection and the Life! I also renounce the blasphemous kissing of the Bible on a witchcraft oath. I cut off all spirits of death, witchcraft, and deception and in the name of Jesus Christ I pray for the healing of the stomach, gall bladder, womb, liver, and any other organs of my body affected by Masonry, and I ask for a release of compassion and understanding for my family and me.

YORK RITE

I renounce the oaths taken by any of my ancestors or me and the penalties and the curses involved in the York Rite of Freemasonry, including these degrees:

Fourth Degree: Mark Master, the secret word JOPPA, the keystone/mark, and the penalty of having the right ear smote off causing permanent deafness and the right hand chopped off for being an imposter.

Fifth Degree: Past Master, with the penalty of having my tongue split from tip to root.

Sixth Degree: Most Excellent Master, with the penalty of having my breast torn open and vital organs removed and exposed to rot on the dung hill.

Seventh Degree: Holy Royal Arch, its secret words JAH-BU-LON and the penalty of having my brain exposed to the scorching rays of the meridian sun. I renounce false communions or Eucharists, all mockery, skepticism, and unbelief about the redemptive work of Jesus Christ on the cross of Calvary.

Eighth Degree: Royal Master, the oaths, secret words and curses.

Ninth Degree: Select Master, and the penalties of having my hands chopped off to the stumps, my eyes plucked out from their sockets, my body quartered and thrown among the rubbish of the temple.

Tenth Degree: Super Excellent Master and the penalties of having my thumbs cut off, my eyes put out, my body bound in fetters and brass and conveyed captive to a strange land.

Eleventh Degree: Knights Order of the Red Cross and the penalties of having my house torn down, the timbers thereof set up and I being hanged thereon.

Twelfth Degree: Knights Templar, the secret word KEB RAIOTH, and penalty of having my head struck off and placed on the highest spire of Christendom.

Thirteenth Degree: Knights of Malta, the secret word MAHER-SHALAL-HASH-BAZ.

ANCIENT & ACCEPTED SCOTTISH RITE

I renounce the oaths taken by any of my ancestors or me and the curses involved in the Ancient and Accepted Scottish Rite including:

Fourth Degree: Secret Master, the secret word ADONAI, and the penalties of all former degrees.

Fifth Degree: Perfect Master, the secret word MAH-HAH-BONE, and the penalty of being smitten to the earth with a setting maul.

Sixth Degree: Intimate Secretary, the secret word JEHOVAH, and the penalty of having my body dissected, and my vital organs cut into pieces and thrown to the beasts of the field.

Seventh Degree: Provost and Judge, the secret words HIRUM-TITO-CIVI-KY, and the penalty of having my nose cut off.

Eighth Degree: hitendant of the Building, the secret word AKAR-JAI-JAH, and the penalties of having my eyes put out, my body cut in two and my bowels exposed.

Ninth Degree: Elected Knights of the Nine, the secret words NEKAM and NEKAH, and the penalty of having my head cut off and stuck on the highest pole in the East as a monument of my villainy.

Tenth Degree: Illustrious Elect of Fifteen, the secret word of Elignam, and the penalties of having my body opened perpendicularly and horizontally, exposed to the air for eight hours so that flies may prey on it, and for my head to be cut off and placed on the highest pinnacle in the world.

Eleventh Degree: Sublime Knights Elect of the Twelve, the secret word STOLKIN-ADONAI, and the penalty of having my hand cut in twain.

Twelfth Degree: Grand Master Architect, the secret word RAB-BANAIM, and penalties.

Thirteenth Degree: Knight of the Ninth Arch of Solomon, the secret word JEHOVAH, and the penalty my body being given to the beasts of the forest as prey.

Fourteenth Degree: Grand Elect, Perfect and Sublime Mason and the penalty of having my body cut open and my bowels given to vultures for food.

COUNCIL OF PRINCES OF JERUSALEM

I renounce the oaths taken by any of my ancestors or me and the curses involved in the Council of Princes of Jerusalem degrees of Freemasonry.

Fifteenth Degree: Knights of the East and the secret word RAPH-O-DOM.

Sixteenth Degree: Prince of Jerusalem, the secret word TEBET-ADAR, and the penalty of being stripped naked and having my heart pierced with a poininiard.

CHAPTER OF THE ROSE CROIX

I renounce the oaths taken by any of my ancestors or me and the curses involved in the Chapter of the Rose Croix degrees of Freemasonry.

Seventeenth Degree: Knights of the East and West, the secret word, ABADDON, and the penalty of incurring the severe wrath of the Almighty Creator of Heaven and Earth.

Eighteenth Degree: Knight of the Pelican and the Eagle & Sovereign Prince Rose Croix of Heredom, the secret words IGNE NATURA RENOVATUR INTEGRA, and the penalties of being forever deprived of the word, to be perpetually in darkness, my blood continually running from my body, to suffer without intermission the most cruel remorse for the soul, that the bitterest gall mixed with vinegar be my constant drink and the sharpest thorns be my pillow and death on the cross complete my punishment. I renounce and reject the Pelican witchcraft spirit, as well as the occultic influence of the Rosicrucians and the Kabala in this degree. I renounce the claim that the death of Jesus Christ was a "dire calamity," and also the deliberate mockery and twisting of the Christian doctrine of the atonement. I renounce the blasphemy and rejection of the deity of Jesus Christ, and the mockery of the communion taken in this degree, including a biscuit, salt, and white wine.

COUNCIL OF KADOSH

I renounce the oaths taken by any of my ancestors or me and the curses involved in the Council of Kadosh degrees of Freemasonry:

Nineteenth Degree: Grand Pontiff and the secret word EMMANUEL.

Twentieth Degree: Grand Master of Symbolic Lodges, the secret words JEKSON/STOLKIN and the penalties of all former obligations.

Twenty-first Degree: Noachite of Prussian Knight and the secret word PELEG.

Twenty-second Degree: Knight of the Royal Axe and the secret words NOAH-BEZALEEI-SODONIAS.

Twenty-third Degree: Chief of the Tabernacle, the secret words URIEL-JEHOVAH and the penalty that the earth should open up and engulf me up to my neck so I perish.

Twenty-fourth Degree: Prince of the Tabernacle and the penalty that I should be stoned to death and my body left above ground to rot.

Twenty-fifth Degree: Knight of the Brazen Serpent, the secret words MOSES-JOHANNES and the penalty that I have my heart eaten by venomous serpents.

Twenty-sixth Degree: Prince of Mercy, the secret words GOMEL and JEHOVAH-JACHIN, and the penalty of condemnation and spite by the entire universe.

Twenty-seventh Degree: Knight Commander of the Temple, the secret word SOLOMON and the penalty of receiving the severest wrath of God inflicted upon me.

Twenty-eighth Degree: Knight Commander of the Sun, or Prince Adept, the secret word STIBIUM and the penalties of having my tongue thrust through with a red-hot iron, my eyes plucked out, my senses of smelling and hearing removed, my hands cut off and in that condition to be left for voracious animals to devour me, or executed by lightening from heaven.

Twenty-ninth Degree: Grand Scottish Knight of Saint Andrew and the secret words NEKAMAH-FURLAC.

Thirtieth Degree: Council of Kadosh, Grand Pontiff, and Knight of the Black and White Eagle, the secret words EMMANUEL, STIBIUM ALKABAR, PHARASH-KOH and all they mean, with all the former penalties applied.

CONSISTORY OF SUBLIME PRINCES OF THE ROYAL SECRET

I renounce the oaths taken by any of my ancestors or me and the curses involved in the Consistory of Sublime Princes of the Royal Secret degrees of Freemasonry, including:

Thirty-first Degree: Grand Inspector Inquisitor Commander. I renounce all the gods and goddesses of Egypt which are honored in this degree, including Anubis with the ram's head, all sun gods, including Ra, Re, Aten and Osiris; and Isis the sister and wife of Osiris and also the moon goddess. I renounce the mother goddess Diana or Artemas. I renounce the Soul of Cheres, the false symbol of immortality, the Chamber of the Dead, and the false teaching of reincarnation.

Thirty-second Degree: Sublime Prince of the Royal Secret and its secret words PHAAL and PHARASH-KOL. I renounce Masonry's false trinitarian deity, AUM, and its parts: Brahma the creator, Vishnu the preserver and Shiva the destroyer. I renounce the deity of AHURA-MAZDA, the claimed spirit or source of all light, and worship with fire, which is an abomination to God, and the drinking from a human skull in some rites.

Thirty-third Degree: Grand Sovereign Inspector General, the secret words DEMOLAY-HIRAM ABIFF, FREDERICK OF PRUSSIA, MICHA, MACHA, BEALIM, and ADONAI; and its penalties being all the former ones, including having my tongue torn out by its roots. I renounce and forsake the declaration that Lucifer is God. I renounce the cable-tow around the neck. I renounce the death wish that the wine drunk from a human skull should turn to poison and the skeleton whose cold arms are invited if the oath of this degree is violated. I renounce the three infamous assassins of their grand master, which are law, property and religion, and the greed and witchcraft involved in the attempt to manipulate and control the rest of mankind

SHRINERS (This exists in America only)

I renounce the oaths taken by my ancestors or me and the curses and penalties involved in the Ancient Arabic Order of the Nobles of the Mystic Shrine. I renounce the piercing of the eyeballs with a three-edged blade, the flaying of the feet and being forced to walk the hot sands upon the sterile shores of the Red Sea until the flaming sun shall strike me with a livid plague. I renounce the madness, the hoodwink, the mock hanging, the mock beheading, the mock drinking of the blood of the victim, the mock dog urinating on the initiate, and the offering of urine as a commemoration. I renounce the worship of the false god Allah as the god of our fathers.

ALL OTHER DEGREES, SECRET LODGES AND SOCIETIES

I renounce any other secret words, attributing false gods' names to God, and idolatrous symbols, such as:

- the Horus, or All-Seeing Eye, which was the emblem of Osiris (the sun god), the creator worshipped by the ancient Egyptians and passed off on current day Masons as the eye of the one true God;

- the G, which the lower degree Masons are told represents geometry or the Great Architect of the Universe (who upper degree Masons learn is Lucifer) but actually can stand for whatever god one chooses, and in books for the upper degrees means "Generating Principal" (phallus);

- the Blazing Star, actually symbolizes various pagan gods and witchcraft;

- the obelisk, which symbolizes a phallus or penis as an emblem of resurrection (but not Christian resurrection);

- the mark in the form of squares and angles which marks the person for life;

- the point within a circle, which the first three degrees of Masons are taught represents the individual Mason inside the bounds of Masonic duty, but which is revealed to the upper levels Mason to represent the sexual union of Osiris and Isis, signifying the prolific powers of nature;

- the Masonic square and compass which likewise represents the sex act;

- the Apron, a symbol of the Masonic belief that salvation must be earned which is a direct violation of Scripture;

- the jewel or talisman that may have been made from this mark sign and worn at lodge meetings;

- the Shriner's fez, which celebrates the Muslim massacre of 50,000 Christians in the Moroccan city of Fez;

- and all others.

I renounce all allegiances to individuals or organizations that are in conflict with the primary allegiance of my life, Jesus Christ, as revealed in God's word, the Bible.

I ask God to cut off all these curses and their effects on my family and me. In the name of Jesus Christ, I pray for the healing of any area where healing is needed by any of us.

I renounce all the other oaths taken by any of my ancestors or me, the rituals and the curses of every other lodge, degree and order involved in Freemasonry anywhere in the world. These include, in part. Prince Hall Masonry (the lodge structure for American Blacks), the Allied Degrees, the Grand Orient Lodges of France, Italy, Central and South America, the Red Cross of Constantine, the Order of the Secret Monitor, the Masonic Royal Order of Scotland, the Order of Amaranth, and the women's Orders of the Eastern Star, of the Ladies Oriental Shrine, and of the White Shrine of Jerusalem; the girls' Orders of the Daughters of the Eastern Star, the International Orders of Job's Daughters and of the Rainbow; and the boys' Order of De Molay,

I renounce involvement by any of my ancestors or me in all other secret societies with ties to Masonry, such as, Mormonism, the Royal Order of Jesters, the Manchester Unity Order of Oddfellows, the Independent Order of Oddfellows and its women's auxiliary called the International Association of Rebekah Assemblies, Buffalos, Druids, Foresters, Orange, Elks, Moose and Eagles

Lodges, the Ku Klux Klan, the White Supremacy Movement, the Grange, the Woodmen of the World, Riders of the Red Robe, the Knights of Pythias, the Mystic order of the Veiled Prophets of the Enchanted Realm, and their effects on me and all my family. I renounce the New World Order, the One World Government, the Illuminati, the Theosophical Society, Cabala, and any other organizations involved with the Masons in the satanic conspiracy to rule the world.

I renounce the ancient pagan teaching of the First Tracing Board, the Second Tracing Board and the Third Tracing Board used in the ritual of the Blue Lodge. I renounce the pagan ritual of the "Point within a Circle" with all its bondages and phallus worship. I renounce the occultic mysticism of the black and white mosaic checkered floor with the tessellated border and the five-pointed blazing star. I renounce the symbol "G" and its veiled pagan symbolism and bondages. I renounce and utterly forsake the Great Architect Of The Universe, who is revealed in the higher degrees as Lucifer, and his false claim to be the universal fatherhood of God. I also renounce the false claim that Lucifer is the Morning Star and Shining One and

I declare that Jesus Christ is the Bright and Morning Star of Revelation 22:16.

I renounce the All-Seeing Third Eye of Freemasonry, or Horus, in the forehead and the obelisk and their pagan and occult symbolism. I renounce all false communions taken, all mockery of the redemptive work of Jesus Christ on the cross of Calvary, all unbelief, confusion and depression, and all worship of Lucifer as God. I renounce and forsake the lie of Freemasonry that man is not sinful, but just imperfect, and so can redeem himself through good works. I rejoice that the Bible states that I cannot do a single thing to earn my salvation, but that I can only be saved by grace through faith in Jesus Christ and what He accomplished on the cross of Calvary.

Father God, I repent of and seek forgiveness for the sins committed by my ancestors and me

- of walking on unholy ground, including Freemasonry, Mormon, occultic and pagan property dedicated to the worship of false gods;

- for the sin of idolatry committed by my ancestors and me of looking to anyone or anything other than the one true Savior, Jesus Christ, for salvation, rescue, protection, or provision;

- for all subversion of justice practiced by the Freemasons or any other organization to which my ancestors or I belonged;

- for the collaboration of the Freemasons in the satanic conspiracy to rule the world.

Father God, I confess to You that when my ancestors and I complained against You we gave Satan a legal right to put the Destroyer in our bloodlines. And when we rebelled against You and rejected Your rightful place as our God, we gave Satan a legal right to deceive us with all the gods of the gentiles. Some of us committed the sin of idolatry by joining Freemasonry. Even if they (we) joined Freemasonry ignorant of its true nature, we are nevertheless guilty of all of its sins. I acknowledge your justice in putting a curse on our bloodlines for this sin and the many sins that followed either by commission or by allegiance to the organization committing the sins. These sins include, in addition to those already confessed, all of the atrocities of satanic ritual abuse practiced at secret levels of Freemasonry: blasphemous rituals, blood sacrifices, animal and human sacrifices, sexual sacrifices, rape, bestiality, sexual immorality, illegitimate births, breeding babies for the purpose of sacrificing them, torture, murder, violence, and mind control (by ElectroVoltOverLoad, withholding normal love, soul shattering, torture, programming and demonization) of infants and children, plus any others. Thank You for Your mercy toward me when You called me to Yourself and gave me faith to believe in Your Son Jesus' atonement for me on the cross. He was made a curse for me so that I no longer have to live under any curse. I ask You, Father God, in the name of Jesus, to forgive all of this generational iniquity in my bloodlines and cleanse it away so the curses do not come down to me or to my children to a thousand generations. I ask You, Jesus, to cleanse my body, soul, and spirit and to deliver me of all the effects of this generational iniquity.

Now dear Father God, I ask humbly for the blood of Jesus Christ, Your Son, to cleanse me from all these sins I have confessed and renounced, to cleanse my spirit, soul and every part of my body which has been effected by these sins, in Jesus name!

Lord Jesus, I ask You to destroy the spiritual equivalents of the physical objects used in Masonry that I now symbolically remove and give to You.

- the hoodwink (a blindfold)
- the veil of mourning
- the mail around the neck
- the noose, which I cut from around the neck and gather together with the cable-tow running down the body
- the ring of the false Freemasonry marriage covenant, which I renounce, from the ring finger of the right hand
- the chains and bondages of Freemasonry on the body
- the ball and chains from the ankles
- all Freemasonry effects, regalia and armor, especially the apron
- all KKK or other secret organization regalia

I renounce every evil spirit associated with Masonry and witchcraft and all other sins and, in the name of Jesus Christ, I command Satan's evil spirits to be bound up into one, leaving nothing of evil remaining, and to leave me now, touching or banning no one, and to go to the place appointed for you by the Lord Jesus, never to return to me or my family. I claim the promise of God's word that whosoever calls on the name of the Lord shall be delivered. Jesus, I ask to be delivered of every spirit of sickness, infirmity, curse, affliction, addiction, disease or allergy associated with these sins that I have confessed and renounced and I ask You to heal me and my family of all effects they have had.

I surrender to God's Holy Spirit and to no other spirit all the places in my life where these sins have affected me. I ask You, Lord, to fill me with (and baptize me in) Your Holy Spirit now according to the promises in Your word. I take to myself the whole armor of God promised in Ephesians 6 and rejoice in its protection as Jesus surrounds me with His Holy Spirit. I enthrone You in my heart. Lord Jesus, for You are my Lord and Savior, and my source of eternal life. Thank You, Father God, for Your mercy, Your forgiveness and Your love, in the name of Jesus Christ. Amen.[12]

ENDNOTES

1 Covey, Stephen, The Seven Habits of Highly Effective People, 1989, p. 31.

2 Moody, Sept. 1991, p. 6.

3 Ankerberg, John, & Weldon, John, Encyclopedia of New Age Beliefs, John Ankerberg & John Weldon, page 596.

4 Fetcho, Dave, "Yoga," Berkeley, CA: Spiritual Counterfeits Project, 1978.

5 Ankerberg, John & Weldon, John, Encyclopedia of New Age Beliefs, John Ankerberg, 1996, p. 593).

6 **Reiker, Hans The Yoga of Light: Hatha Yoga Pradipika, New York: Seabury Press, 1971.**

7 Ankerberg, John & Weldon, John, Encyclopedia of New Age Beliefs, p. 17.

8 Wolman, B., Benjamin, Ullman, Mantague, eds., Benjamin B. Wolman, Handbook of States of Consciousness, New York: Van Nostrand Reinhold, 1986.

9 Liveprayer Daily Devotional, Bill Keller radio broadcast.

10 Cox, Paul, Guidelines to Deliverance, pp. 128-129, used by permission.

11 Declarations and prayer by Dr. Mike Hutchings, used by permission. Dr. Hutchings desires, for who are willing, to send him testimonies of those who were healed through the use of his prayer model. Send testimonies to mikeh@globalawakening.com.

12 This material was adapted by Karen Sackett, of Shield of Faith

Ministries, Minneapolis, MN, and further modified by lay counselors at Christ Church Evangelical Presbyterian Church, Anderson, SC. The original "Prayer of Release for Masons and Their Descendants" is contained in the book Unmasking Freemasonry, Removing the Hoodwink, by Selwyn Stevens, ISBN 0-9583417-3-7, and combined with information from Greg Lambert's book. Masonic Symbolism Explained. ISBN 1-877203-04-1, both of which can be obtained through Jubilee Publishers, P.O. Box 36-044, Wellington 6330, New Zealand, or by visiting their Internet site, www.jubilee.org.nz, where additions are made to the prayer periodically

Don't Forget!

*Get the most from this series
by purchasing your copy of
these companion books*

www.ingramcontent.com/pod-product-compliance
Lightning Source LLC
Chambersburg PA
CBHW032047090426
42744CB00004B/116